Jibber Jabber & Giffle Gaffle

A Collection of Salacious Slang and
Popular Profanities Through the Ages

Elanor Clarke

summersdale

CONTENTS

INTRODUCTION

Most of us would not claim to have a perfect grasp of the 'Queen's English', so it may be some consolation to learn just how much slang is used in everyday conversations. Slights, slang and profanities have made up a significant part of the English language for hundreds of years, from the code-like terms of the canting crew, up to modern-day reworkings of rhyming slang, and the antiquities which are still used by a large number of people, who likely don't realise just how old these words are. Some have disappeared and then made a comeback, parading as something new, while others have changed meaning altogether, or completely vanished.

Slang is expressive. It can be vulgar, offensive, comical, entertaining. While this collection contains a good many forgotten gems, it also provides a little history for some of the everyday terms many love to use. It may be surprising to discover just how many 'rude' words started out life as standard English, before Victorian prudery confined them to the realm of the taboo.

The material in this book is by no means exhaustive; rather it gives a considered but somewhat tongue-in-cheek (in the spirit of the most amusing and enduring slang words and phrases) overview of old vernacular, with lively descriptions which help to frame the word, and perhaps even help you put it to use! Read it cover to cover, or dip in to the sections you like the sound of – either way, I hope you enjoy these peculiarities and vulgarities as much as I have enjoyed writing about them.

Elanor Clarke, 2013

Everyday Words and Phrases

PEOPLE
Or Bacon, Breadbaskets and Bums

THE ALTOGETHER *n.* 19th century. To be 'in the buff'; 'starkers', i.e. nude. From 'altogether naked', therefore completely without clothing.

ARSE *n.* The posterior or rump. Although around since approximately the 10th century, coming from Old German into standard English, this term only became slang, and considered offensive, in the mid-17th century. Alternatively spelt 'ass', and was in this form often used by Old Bill the Bard himself. Still in common usage.

BACON *n.* 16th century. One's physical person, i.e. the body, used by Falstaff in *Henry IV*. Still in use within modern terms such as 'to save your own bacon', meaning to save your life.

BEAK *n.* Schnozz; sniffer; konk, i.e. the nose. Often used as an insult, to describe an overly large or hooked snout. Common from 19th century but used as early as the 16th century. Still in common usage.

BEER BARREL *n.* 19th century. The dark, voluminous receptacle of ale, i.e. the stomach, after its capacity to hold grog and other such liquid delights. Also, the body as a whole.

BELLY *n.* 10th century. The bread bin; the gut; the stomach. With varied European roots, all of which mean 'sack' or 'bag'. Considered particularly vulgar from around 1840, but tame in the modern tongue.

"CABOOSE"
n. 19th century.
The rear end; buttocks.

BILLY-GOAT *n.* 19th century. A man with a tufted chin or jawline, after the bearded appearance of a male goat.

BIRTHDAY SUIT *n.* 18th century. The bare body; the perfectly fitting 'suit' you're wearing when you are born. First used by author Tobias Smollett in *The Adventures of Ferdinand, Count Fathom* in 1753. Still in common usage.

BONE-HOUSE *n.* 19th century. A place where one's skeleton dwells, i.e. the body. A morbid description of a person's physical make-up.

BREADBASKET *n.* 18th century. The belly; the gut; the stomach, after its prime purpose; to be filled with bread and other such staples.

BUM *n.* Breech; backside; buttocks. Used as early as the 14th century, this term is still in common use.

CABOOSE *n.* 19th century. The rear end; buttocks. Derived from the word for the rear part of a coach or railway train.

CHALK FARM *n.* 19th century. Rhyming slang for 'arm'.

DINING ROOM FURNITURE *n.* 19th century. Pearly white items which furnish the mouth, i.e. teeth.

FOREFOOT *n.* 16th century. Hand. Compares the human hand to an animal's anatomy. Popularised by the works of Old Bill himself.

GOB *n.* The yawning gateway to the alimentary canal, i.e. the mouth, from the Gaelic meaning 'beak'. Often used negatively, e.g. in the phrase 'shut your gob'. In continuous usage since the 14th century.

GRAVEYARD *n.* 19th century. The site where miniature 'tombstones' are placed, all in a row, i.e. the mouth.

HATCHWAY *n.* 19th century. The sometimes creaking entranceway to the breadbasket, i.e. the mouth.

LEADING ARTICLE *n.* 19th century. The foremost point on the face, i.e. the nose.

MAG *n*. 18th century. A gossip. An abbreviation of magpie, a bird which has a bad reputation that suggests its chatter is a bad omen.

MEDLAR *n*. 17th century. The brown-eye, the arsehole; the anus. Inspired by the fruit which has a star-like opening revealing brown innards, and is often referred to as the 'dog's arse fruit' or 'open arse fruit'.

MOUSER *n*. 19th century. Moustache, for its furriness. Also a woman's pubic hair. See also MUFF.

MUFF *n*. 19th century. A hairy soup-strainer i.e. a 'tache. Also a woman's bush (pubic hair). Still in use with the second meaning.

MUG *n.* 18th century. A person's visage; the face, possibly in response to the drinking mugs designed to look like grotesque faces which were available at the time. Still in common usage, especially as 'ugly mug'.

PAW *n.* 16th century. Hand. Compares the human hand to an animal's anatomy. Still in common usage, e.g. in the phrase 'keep your paws off'.

PINS *n, pl.* Legs. 16th century. Pin, at the time, primarily meant 'peg'. Still in common usage.

PORTHOLE *n.* 17th century. The winker; the bum hole; the anus. Likely referencing the shape of the opening.

PRAT *n.* 17th century. The backside; the arse; the buttocks. Still in common usage, but now generally as an insult with a meaning similar to 'idiot'.

PUDDING-HOUSE *n.* 18th century. A lodge for cake and other such culinary delights i.e. the stomach.

RING *n.* 19th century. The anal sphincter, after the shape of the muscle. Still in common usage.

"PUDDING-HOUSE" n. 18th century. A lodge for cake.

SENSITIVE TRUNCHEON *n.* 19th century. The nose. Truncheon suggests a large nose, and sensitive possibly because it is one of the first things to feel the cold, possibly because it is easily broken.

SHINER *n.* 19th century. A black eye. Still in common usage.

SPEW ALLEY *n.* 18th century. The dark, stinking passageway through which the contents of one's stomach may pass during illness, i.e. the throat, 'spew' being 'vomit'.

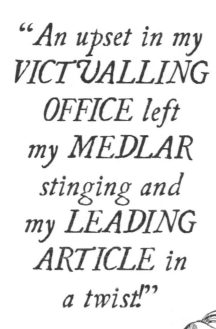

"*An upset in my*
VICTUALLING
OFFICE left
my MEDLAR
stinging and
my LEADING
ARTICLE in
a twist!"

VICTUALLING OFFICE – Stomach
MEDLAR – Anus
LEADING ARTICLE – Nose

STAMPS *n, pl.* 16th century. Legs. Directly taken from their use in walking, or stamping around.

STROMMEL *n.* 16th century. Hair. From the German word, this literally means straw.

VICTUALLING OFFICE *n.* 19th century. Stomach. After its capacity for being filled with food.

BODILY FUNCTIONS
Or Tom Turdman in
the Crapping castle

BOG *n.* 18th century. The place you go to evacuate the ponging contents of your lower intestine, i.e. the toilet. Still in common usage. See also BOGGARD.

BOGGARD *n.* 16th century. The crapper; the pot; the toilet. Gave rise to several other slang terms, including the 17th-century term BOGHOUSE, and the enduring BOG.

CRAPPER *n.* 18th century. Toilet. One of the most enduring terms for the privy, and still in common use, this word focusses on its purpose as a receptacle for excrement (crap).

CRAPPING CASTLE *n.* 18th century. The porcelain throne, i.e. the toilet. Derived from CRAPPER, this term alludes to the idea of the 'king' or 'queen' sitting on the 'throne' in his or her 'castle' – a euphemism which is still in common usage. The man who invented the flushing toilet was, somewhat fittingly, named Crapper.

TO DRAIN THE DRAGON *v.* 19th century. To dispel yellow elixir from one's 'trouser beast', i.e. to piss (specifically male urination, the dragon being the penis.)

GONG *n.* 11th century. The place where one answers the call of nature, i.e. the toilet. Also seen as 'gong house', this is one of the earliest words for the lavatory. From the Old English *gang*, which means 'going'. Indeed, people will still say 'I need to go!'

GRAVESEND SWEETMEATS *n, pl.* 17th century. Inconsumable Kentish delicacy, i.e. solid pieces of sewage, excrement. Referencing the sewer system of the time. Later, by the 19th century, it had changed meaning and was used to describe shrimp!

TO BE HARD-BAKED *v.* 19th century. To overcook the colon casserole; to be constipated. Related to the term 'best let it bake', when one needs to defecate but cannot.

JERE-PECK *n.* 17th century. A sewer. From 'jere', meaning *turd*, and 'peck', a heap.

LONG TEA *n.* 18th century. The yellow-brown contents of the bladder, not brewed for drinking, i.e. piss. Sometimes seen as just 'tea'. See also TEA VOIDER.

"MEMBER MUG"
n. 17th century.
A receptacle for the
tallywhacker.

TO BE LOOSE IN THE HILT *n.* 19th century. To be prone to an explosive outburst from one's breech, i.e. to have diarrhoea. References the 'looseness' of the stools and/or the anus.

MEMBER MUG *n.* 17th century. A receptacle for the tallywhacker and its steaming effluence, i.e. a chamber pot.

PISS *n.* Urine. An onomatopoeic term, in use since the 13th century, but considered slang from the Victorian era onwards. Still in common usage.

PISSPOT *n*. Chamber pot. A portable pissoir; a potty. A literal description of its purpose, which was standard English from the 15th century, but became slang and considered vulgar in the 18th century. The phrase 'haven't got a pot to piss in', meaning poor, with no possessions, is still in use.

PLEASURE GARDEN PADLOCK *n*. 19th century. A menstrual cloth, the 'pleasure garden' being the vagina, and it being 'locked', not useable for sex, during the woman's period.

SNOT *n*. 15th century. Yellow-green slime which flows from the fleshy fount in the middle of one's face, i.e. nasal mucus. From the 12th-century term 'snite', which means to wipe the nose. Still in common usage.

TO TAP A KEG *v.* 19th century. To syphon a draft from the piss barrel, i.e. to urinate. Linking urination to alcohol, specifically the beer trade.

TOM TURDMAN *n.* 17th-century name given to the latrine man, whose job it was to empty people's toilets before the flushing toilet was invented.

TURD *n.* Excrement. From the Old English word *tord*, this term has been in use since the 10th century. It refers to the way excrement leaves the body, meaning tear or split. Considered ruder after the mid-13th century, it became slang around the mid-18th century. Still in common usage, also as an insult or term of derision.

TO WHIP THE CAT *v.* 17th century. To vomit.

"Got his SIT-DOWN-UPONS and HOWDY'E DOS covered with GRAVESEND SWEETMEATS. What a stink!"

SIT-DOWN-UPONS – *Trousers*
HOWDY'E DOS – *Shoes*
GRAVESEND SWEETMEATS
– *Excrement*

ANIMALS AND INSECTS
Or Tits and Cheats

BOSOM FRIENDS *n*, *pl*. 19th century. Parasitic insects; lice, from their proximity to the skin.

CACKLING-CHETE *n*. 16th century. Chicken. A logical name which literally means 'cackling thing'. See also QUACKING CHEAT.

CHATES *n*, *pl*. 18th century. Lice. Also seen as 'chats'. Developed from the word 'chattels', meaning livestock or other property which could be moved from place to place.

CHICKABIDDY *n.* 19th century. Nursery term for chicken; also a term of endearment for a young child.

DAISY-CUTTER *n.* 18th century. A slovenly horse. The pejorative form of 'daisy-kicker', this suggests a horse which will not raise its feet properly when walking or running, therefore cutting down the flowers in its field with its hooves.

DOBBIN *n.* 16th century. A nag. This refers to a normal farm horse, but may also be used for an old or broken-down horse. One of the earliest uses of the word is in 1596, in Bill the Bard's *The Merchant of Venice*.

FEN NIGHTINGALE *n.* 19th century. Frog. From the noise a frog makes, particularly in the evening. Also referred to as 'Cambridge nightingale'.

LONG-FACED CHUM *n.* 19th century. Horse. Coined by the British Army; for a soldier, a good horse would have been a best friend in times of need.

MACARONI *n.* 19th century. Rhyming slang for 'pony'.

PARTLET *n.* 15th century. Chicken. From the French *pertelote*, which was also the standard English term for a short time.

QUACKING CHEAT *n.* 16th century. Duck. Like *cackling-chete*, which emphasises the noise made by a chicken, this term focusses on the quacking of the duck, 'cheat' simply meaning 'thing'.

TO BE SILER-LACED *v.* 19th century. To be lousy, from the perceived colour of lice.

TIT *n.* 16th century. A small, usually female, horse. It is from this term that 'tit' came to be used to mean a young woman.

"MACARONI"
n. 19th century. Rhyming slang for 'pony'.

THINGS
Or Fleshbags, Louse-traps and Slap

BARNACLES *n, pl.* 16th century. Specs; blinkers; glasses. From the 14th-century term 'barnacle', which denoted a type of bit which pinched the nose of the horse, the same way early spectacles pinched the nose of the wearer.

BEES AND HONEY *n.* 18th/19th century. Rhyming slang for 'money'. Seen also as 'bread and honey'.

BEETLE-CRUSHERS *n, pl.* 19th century. Footwear which poses a threat to the general wellbeing of beetles and other such crawling creatures, i.e. boots – though the word originally meant feet. Either way, named for the heavy footsteps of a clod-hopping human being.

BOB *n.* 18th century. A shilling. The phrase 'ten bob' is still in usage and now means fifty pence, the modern equivalent value of ten shillings.

BOUNG *n.* 16th century. A purse or *pocket*. Seen also as 'bung'. From the Frisian word *pung*, meaning purse.

BRASS *n.* Moolah; bread; money. From its metallic make-up. In continuous use since the 16th century, although the actual make up of coins has changed over the centuries.

BUM-FREEZER *n.* 19th century. A short jacket, so called due to the fact it wouldn't cover the wearer's bum. Seen also as 'bum-cooler' and 'bum-perisher'.

"BUM-FREEZER"
n. 19th century.
A short jacket.

CARRIONCASE *n.* 19th century. A fabric vessel in which to encase your flesh, i.e. a shirt. From its closeness to the torso. See also FLESHBAG.

CASE *n.* 19th century. A counterfeit crown. Also seen as 'caser'.

CLOBBER *n.* 19th century. Vestments; apparel; clothing. Developed from Yiddish. Still in common usage.

COVER-ME-DECENT *n.* 19th century. A garment which preserves one's dignity, i.e. coat (which covers much of the body). Seen also as 'cover-me-decently'.

DAISY ROOTS *n, pl*. 19th century. Rhyming slang for 'boots'.

DISHABILLY *n*. 18th century. Disrobed; clothes-less; nude. From the French term *en déshabillé*, meaning undressed.

TO BE DRESSED WITHIN AN INCH OF ONE's LIFE *v*. 19th century. To be clothed excessively sharply; to be well-dressed.

EEL-SKINS *n*. 19th century. Excessively tight trousers which cling to the wearer's legs, like the skin clings to an eel's body.

EXCRUCIATORS *n, pl*. 19th century. Tight, pointed shoes, named for the way they would painfully pinch the wearer's feet. Related to the 20th-century fashion shoe, the 'winkle-picker'.

FARTING CRACKERS *n*. 17th century. Legwear which bears the brunt of the draft from a person's back passage, i.e. trousers; originally meant breeches.

FIVE POT PIECE *n*. 19th century. A half-crown. A term used by medical students, which refers to the price of a pot of HALF AND HALF at the pub.

FLESHBAG *n*. 19th century. Shirt, after its closeness to the body. Literally a bag in which to hold your own flesh. See also CARRIONCASE.

FRILLERY *n*. 19th century. Undercrackers; knicks; pants, i.e. underwear, from its delicate and/or frilly design.

GINGERBREAD *n*. 17th century. Gold. From its yellow colour, and possibly because to have gold would be 'sweet'.

GOLDFINCH *n.* 18th/19th century. A golden guinea. See also YELLOW HAMMER, named for a bird both for its golden feathers and the way the money would so easily be spent, as if 'flying' away.

HAM-BAGS *n.* 19th century. Wrapping for the 'hams', i.e. ladies' knickers.

HOCK-DOCKIES *n, pl.* 18th century. Shoes. From 'hock', a horse's leg, and 'dock', i.e. a space to install one's hooves.

"HAM-BAGS"
n. 19th century. Ladies' knickers.

HOWDY'E DOS *n*, *pl.* 19th century. Rhyming slang for 'shoes'.

HOXTER *n.* 19th century. An inside pocket. From the Northern dialect 'oxter', which means the armpit, this word emphasises the position of the pocket.

LOOR *n.* 14th century. The oldest slang term for money. Contemporary synonyms include 'Lowrie' and 'lurries'. From the French *lower* meaning wages or takings, and the Romany *lowe*, which means to plunder.

LOUSE TRAP *n.* 18th century. A comb. Needing a louse trap suggests dirty hair.

MISH-TOPPER *n.* 17th century. A coat or cloak, an item which one puts on top of a 'mish' or shirt.

MONMOUTH STREET FINERY *n.* 19th century. Second-hand clothes, after Monmouth Street, which was the centre of the trade in second-hand clothes. Charles Dickens referred to the area as 'the burial place of fashion'.

MUCKENDER *n.* 18th century. A handy rag used to remove muck from the end of the schnozz, i.e. a handkerchief. The word was originally used to mean a swab.

To PUT ON DOG *v.* 19th century. To get dressed, especially to dress smartly. From 'doggy', meaning 'stylish'.

QUEEN'S PICTURES *n.* 19th century. Dosh; money, from the fact that the Queen's face is printed on all British currency.

QUID *n.* 17th century. One pound sterling is a 'quid', though at first it was used to mean 'monarch'. Possibly from the Latin *quid* meaning 'what', this would originally have had 'one needs' as a suffix but this has subsequently been dropped. Still in common usage.

RAGGERY *n.* 17th century. Ladies' clothing, rags being all clothes, not just ragged ones.

ROGER *n.* 17th century. A pocket, though the term originally meant a suitcase.

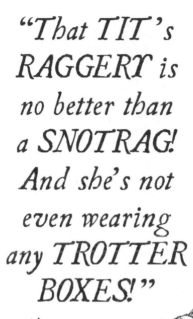

"That *TIT*'s *RAGGERY* is no better than a *SNOTRAG*! And she's not even wearing any *TROTTER BOXES*!"

TIT – *A young girl*
RAGGERY – *Clothes*
SNOTRAG – *Handkerchief*
TROTTER BOXES – *Shoes*

"SWEETPEA"
n. 19th century.
Urine.

SAUSAGE AND MASH *n.* 18th/19th century. Rhyming slang for cash. This is where the phrase 'not a sausage', meaning nothing, especially no money, originated. 'Not a sausage' is still in common usage.

SHIMMY *n.* 19th century. Shirt. Developed from *commission*, which in turn came from the Italian-influenced *camesa*.

SIT-DOWN-UPONS *n, pl.* 19th century. Arse-cushioning vestment, i.e. trousers.

SLAP *n.* Make-up, 19th-century theatrical term, likely from the way it was applied to the face. Still in common usage.

SLOPS *n, pl*. 19th century. Clothing; at first only a sailor's ready-made uniform, but later also used for any clothing.

SNAKE IN THE GRASS *n*. 19th century. Rhyming slang for 'glass', either a looking glass or a drinking glass, for the fact that either could turn out to be a false friend.

SNOTRAG *n*. 19th century. Handkerchief, for its use in blowing or wiping the nose. Still in common usage, though now the word can be applied to any tissue or cloth which has been used to wipe or blow the nose.

SWEETPEA *n*. 19th century. Urine. Usually used when referencing a lady relieving herself in the open, e.g. on a walk in the countryside.

TEARS OF THE TANKARD *n.* 17th century. Stains on the clothes from drink.

TEA VOIDER *n.* 18th century. One who is urinating, for the tea-like colour of urine, and the voiding of the bladder. See also LONG TEA.

THREPS *n.* 17th century. A threepenny bit, from the way it was pronounced (threpenny).

THRUMBUSKINS *n.* 18th century. A threepenny bit, from the 'three' part of the word.

TILBURY *n.* 18th century. A silver sixpence. This name references the cost of the ferry across the Thames between Gravesend in Kent and Tilbury Fort in Essex.

TIT *n.* 16th century. A young girl. Later became a word for breast, see TITS.

TROTTER-BOXES *n, pl.* 19th century. Hoof encasements, i.e. shoes. Also seen as 'trotter-cases'. From 'trotter' meaning foot, and comparing the human foot to an animal one, and 'box' or 'case', something in which to store said trotter.

TOGS *n.* Clothing. In continuous use since the 14th century. Related to the Latin *toga*.

WEDGE *n.* 18th century. Silver. This term has been revived during modern times and has come to mean money in general.

"*Young Will can't help but WAG THE RED RAG. He's only gone and BLOWN THE GAFF! Now the COPPERS are sure to be on to us.*"

WAG THE RED RAG – Blabber
BLOW THE GAFF – Spill the beans
COPPERS – Police

WHISTLING BREECHES *n.* 19th century. Noisy trousers, specifically corduroys, for the sound they make when the wearer walks.

WRAP-RASCAL *n.* 18th century. A red cloak. Likely from the idea that red was a devilish colour.

YELLOW HAMMER *n.* 18th/19th century. A golden guinea. Named after the golden-coloured bird, possibly for the way the money would 'fly'. See also GOLDFINCH.

YENNOP *n.* 19th century. Backslang for penny. Seen also as 'yennep' and 'yennap'.

MISCELLANEOUS
Or Random Giffle Gaffle

TO BLOW THE GAFF *v*. 19th century. To spill the beans; to tell a secret.

GIFFLE GAFFLE *n.* 19th century. Nonsense; from the Icelandic *gafla*.

TO GIVE GREEN RATS *v*. 19th century. To talk about someone behind their back, to slander someone, to backbite. The use of 'green' suggests envy.

JABBER *n.* 16th century. Gossip or idle chatter. From the word 'jibb', the tongue. Still in use, but more often to mean incoherent talk, or indeed incessant chatter.

SOFT SAWDER *n.* 19th century. Flattery, 'sawder' being solder, which is used to smooth things out.

TO TALK THE HIND LEGS OFF A DONKEY *v.* 19th century. To talk too much, to the point of boredom, and/or to talk too fast. Still in use, though often with another animal's legs, such as a horse.

TO WAFFLE *v.* 19th century. To talk too much and/or to talk rubbish. Originally a printers' term, which meant nonsense. Still in common usage.

"TO WAG THE RED RAG"
v. 17th century. To chatter.

TO WAG THE RED RAG *v*. 17th century. To chatter, the red rag being the tongue.

TO YAFFLE *v*. 19th century. To talk incoherently and/or too fast. From the Yorkshire dialect, meaning to mumble or yelp.

YAP *v*. 19th century. To waffle, to prattle on and speak too much. Still in use, especially for the noise made by a small dog.

SUSTENANCE

FOOD
Or Belly Furniture

BAGS OF MYSTERY *n.* 19th century. Unidentifiable meat encased in pigs' guts, i.e. sausages, for the way they are produced (the skin being a 'bag') and the fact that you never really know what's in them! A name showing distrust for the food's contents. See also CHAMBERS OF HORRORS.

BEEMAL *n.* 18th/19th century. Lamb. Butchers' backslang which was predominantly used to disguise when customers were being sold inferior cuts of meat. Other examples would be 'feeb' for beef, and 'kayrop' for pork. Not strictly backwards, letters were added or taken away to make the word more pronounceable and/or harder for the layman to understand.

BELLY CHERE *n.* 17th century. Nosh; grub. Can be spelt 'belly cheer', after the idea that a full stomach is a happy stomach.

BELLY FURNITURE *n.* 17th century. Edibles with which one furnishes one's gut, i.e. food.

BURGOO *n.* 18th century. Oat porridge, from the Turkish word *burghal*, which means cracked wheat (bulgur wheat).

CACKLING FART *n.* 16th century. Egg. From the cackling sound made by a chicken, and the way that eggs are laid.

"CHUFF"
n. 19th century.
Fodder.

CHAMBERS OF HORRORS *n.* 19th century. Stomach-churning, grimace-inducing bangers, i.e. sausages. For the way they are formed, as filled skins, and the fact that horrific ingredients may be used in the filling. Shows a distrust of the food based on its ingredients. See also BAGS OF MYSTERY.

CHOW *n.* 19th century. Edibles. Originally from Chinese pidgin, and meaning a mixture, which became a word for food in general. Still in common usage, especially in 'chow mein'.

CHUFF *n.* 19th century. Fodder. A derivative of *chow.* In modern slang, 'to chuff' is often used to mean 'to fart', or 'to be chuffed' is to be pleased.

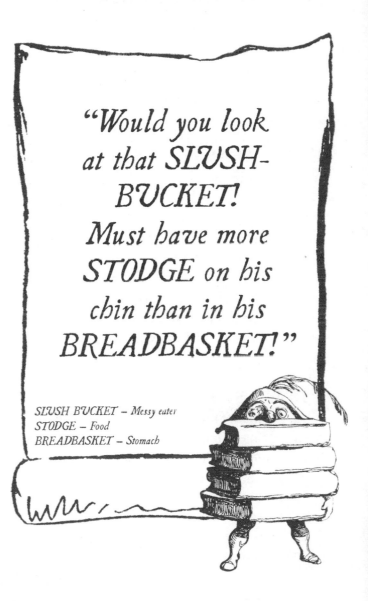

"Would you look at that SLUSH-BUCKET! Must have more STODGE on his chin than in his BREADBASKET!"

SLUSH BUCKET – Messy eater
STODGE – Food
BREADBASKET – Stomach

DOGSBODY *n.* 19th century. A stew, specifically pease pudding.

FANNY ADAMS *n.* 19th century. Tinned mutton, from naval slang. Named after an eight-year-old girl who was murdered in 1867. Her body was cut to pieces and it was this detail that led servicemen, unhappy with the quality of their mutton, to suggest it was Fanny Adams' remains. Her name has lasted in British slang, with 'sweet FA' now meaning 'nothing at all', and naval mess tins or cooking pots still known as 'Fannys'.

FIDDLER'S FARE *n.* 18th century. The payment for a fiddler's work, being meat, drink (likely wine) and money. An improvement on the 17th-century 'fiddler's pay', which was wine and thanks, and the 16th-century 'fiddler's wages', which meant thanks alone.

GOD'S MERCY *n.* 19th century. A meal of bacon (or ham) and eggs, for the grace that might be said before eating.

GRUB *n.* 17th century. Food. Also used as a verb, to eat, or to beg for food. Reminiscent of grubbing around for food, the way a pig would, this term is still in common usage, especially in phrases such as 'grub's up!', meaning dinner is ready.

GRUBBING-KEN *n.* 19th century. An eating house, 'grubbing' being eating, and 'ken' being a place or house.

GRUNTING-PECK *n.* 16th century. Pork. Literally means 'grunting food' or 'grunting meat'. Also seen as 'grunter'.

IRISH APRICOTS *n.* 19th century. Potatoes. After their position as the staple food in Ireland. Also seen as 'Irish lemons'.

LOBLOLLY *n.* 16th century. A thick gruel. From 'lob', which means bubbling or boiling. This word was also used to mean a ship's doctor's medicines.

MANARVEL *v.* 19th century. Related to MANAVILINS, this term was used by the navy to describe the theft of small stores. As a noun, it was more widely used to mean small change.

MANAVILINS *n.* 19th century. Bits and pieces of meat, a similar meaning to CHOW. Also seen as 'manablins'.

MUNGA *n*. 19th century. Munch; chow; sustenance. From the French *manger* and the Italian *mangiare*, both of which mean 'to eat'. Can also be spelt 'munger', 'mungy' or 'mungarly'.

MUNGARLY-CASA *n*. 19th century. A baker's shop. 'Mungarly' usually refers to food in general, but here it is used more specifically.

MUNGY-WALLAH *n*. 19th century. From the armed forces, this term meant a man who worked in the cookhouse.

NEEDLE AND THREAD *n*. 19th century. Rhyming slang for 'bread'.

PECK *n*. 16th century. That which one buries one's beak in, i.e. food, or meat. From the pecking of birds when they eat.

TO TAKE A HOLIDAY AT PECKHAM *v.* 16th century. To have nothing to eat, punning on 'peck'.

POOR MAN'S TREACLE *n.* In the 17th century, this referred to garlic, but by the 19th century it referred to onions.

ROOTI *n.* 19th century. Bread. A word used by the British Army, taken from the Hindi word *roti*, which is a type of unleavened bread.

SERGEANT MAJOR *n.* 19th century. A plump loin of mutton, named for the fatness of a sergeant major, who would likely lead an easy, well-fed lifestyle, and for the streaks of fat in the meat, which bear a resemblance to his stripes.

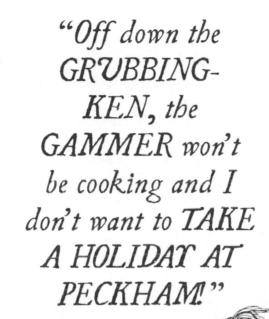

"Off down the **GRUBBING-KEN,** *the* **GAMMER** *won't be cooking and I don't want to* **TAKE A HOLIDAY AT PECKHAM!"**

GRUBBING KEN – Eatery
GAMMER – Wife
TAKE A HOLIDAY AT PECKHAM
– Go hungry

SHARP'S ALLEY BLOOD WORMS *n.*
19th century. Sausages. Named for Sharp's
Alley, an abattoir near London's Smithfield
meat market. Also refers to the large amount
of blood found in sausages, particularly
specialities like black pudding. Another
term which shows distaste for this food's
ingredients, like BAGS OF MYSTERY or
CHAMBERS OF HORRORS.

SLUSH-BUCKET *n.* 19th century. A messy
eater, one with bad manners. Slush was a
word for fat and fatty food. This term
suggests someone whose food, or fat, is
spilling out of their mouth as they eat.

SMASH *n.* 19th century. Mashed turnips, for
the way they are broken up in the mashing
process. Still used today, but as a brand
name for instant mashed potatoes.

SNOB'S DUCK *n.* 19th century. A leg of lamb filled with a stuffing of sage and onions. 'Snob' here does not refer to someone who acts like they are superior to others, but rather to a cobbler, meaning this posh-sounding dish is actually poor people's food.

SPOTTED DOG *n.* 19th century. A dumpling with plums or currants, the fruit being the 'spots'. Similar to SPOTTED DICK.

"SLUSH-BUCKET"
n. 19th century. A messy eater.

SPOTTED DICK *n*. 19th century. A sweet suet pudding with currants or raisins, often served with custard. The name is possibly derived from SPOTTED DOG, or from the latter part of pudding. Spotted dick is still eaten today, and so the term is still widely used.

STAGGERING BOB *n*. 19th century. Meat which is not fit for human consumption, often associated with the meat of an animal which has died, therefore staggered around, rather than being butchered.

STICK IN THE RIBS *n*. 19th century. Thick soup which refuses to pass easily into the breadbasket. Nowadays in US cooking terminology, 'stick to the ribs food' is used to describe homey or fatty, comforting food.

STODGE *n.* 19th century. Food, particularly thick and/or fatty food. Still used today, especially adjectivally as stodgy, mainly to describe foods such as stews and puddings.

WABBLER *n.* 19th century. Also seen spelt 'wobbler'. A boiled leg of mutton, likely named for the way its fat becomes gelatinous and wobbly when boiled.

DRINK
Or Lap

ACT OF PARLIAMENT *n.* 18th century. Sub-standard hogswill (particularly, small beer) provided by the government to the British Army for free.

BELCH *n.* 19th century. A gassy, sour-tasting excuse for beer which causes undue belching.

BELLY-VENGEANCE *n.* 19th century. Stomach-churning ale which induces one's guts to take revenge in the form of vomit and/or explosive excrement.

BENDER *n.* 19th century. A drinking binge. Still in common usage, with people referring to someone 'going on a bender' if they have indulged in excessive alcohol consumption.

BENBOUSE *n.* 19th century. Beer, especially good-quality beer. Literally means 'good drink'.

BEVVY *n.* 19th century. Beer, or an alcoholic drink in general. From the Latin *bibere*, to drink. Possibly an abbreviation of beverage, a drink. Can also be used to mean a public house. Still in common usage.

BEVVY MERCHANT *n.* 19th century. A consummate piss-artist; a drunk, or a heavy drinker, rather than someone who sells drinks.

"BUNGJUICE"
n. 19th century. Libation
from a stoppered container,
particularly ale.

BOB *n.* 18th century. Gin. One of the many slang names given to this extremely popular drink, and also a term for a large beer jug which holds a gallon. Also seen as 'royal bob'.

BOOZE *n.* 16th century. The drink that brings happiness and headaches, i.e. alcohol. Also used as a verb, to booze, meaning to drink excessively. Also appeared as early as the 14th century, though with the meaning of a drinking vessel, rather than of the drink, or act of drinking, itself. Most likely from the German term *buzen*, which means to drink excessively. The term is still in common usage, as a noun and a verb, including pubs often being referred to as 'boozers', a term which can also apply to a drunk.

TO BE BOWSERED *v.* 16th century. To be inebriated as a result of consuming copious amounts of booze.

BRITISH CHAMPAGNE *n.* 19th century. Fizz for the rank and file, i.e. beer. A development from the earlier *English burgundy*, suggesting beer is the equivalent speciality to the enduringly popular champagne.

BUMPER *n.* 17th century. An overflowing tankard; a full glass (of an alcoholic drink).

BUNGJUICE *n.* 19th century. Libation from a stoppered container, particularly ale. From the bung used to cap a beer barrel.

CAT'S WATER *n.* 19th century. Gin. From the name of a well-known distiller, 'Old Tom', tom being a male cat. 'Old Tom' could also be used as a term for gin. Also suggests a strong drink (from the strong smell of cat pee). The modern term 'cat's piss' likely came from this, though it now means a weak, watery or unappetising drink.

CINDER *n.* 19th century. Any strong alcoholic drink which has been mixed with water, tea or lemonade.

COLD TEA *n.* 17th century. Brandy, from its tea-like colour.

COMBOOZELATED *adj.* 19th century. Sozzled; pissed; drunk – derived from 'booze'.

COOLER *n.* 19th century. Beer drunk after spirits, for the way it would 'cool' the mouth and throat.

CORPSE REVIVER *n.* 19th century. A hangover cure. From the half-dead feeling one would have after overindulging, the body or 'corpse' would therefore need reviving. 'Reviver' on its own is also seen as a word for an alcoholic drink, comparing alcohol to medicine or a health-giving tonic.

TO BE IN ONE'S CUPS *v.* To be drunk. Slang between the 16th and the 18th century, before it became standard English.

TO BECOME CUPSHOT *v.* 16th century. To be 'shot' dead, therefore passed out, from the cup, full of alcohol, i.e. drunk.

DANDY *n.* 19th century. A small tumbler used for drinking alcohol, specifically punch.

TO DISGUISE ONESELF *v.* 16th century. To drink enough alcohol as to contrive one's visage to the point at which it is no longer one's own, i.e. become very drunk.

TO GO DOWN WITH BARREL FEVER *v.* 18th century. To fall into a red-eyed, mumbling state of illness and confusion due to excessive consumption of grog.

ENGLISH BURGUNDY *n.* 18th century. Beer. Burgundy was a popular drink, and beer was seen as the English equivalent speciality. See also BRITISH CHAMPAGNE.

EYE WATER *n.* 19th century. Tear-inducing gin.

FLASH *n.* 18th century. A drink. Though technically a general term, this was most often used to mean gin, in which case it can also be seen as 'flash of lightning', which is directly related to another gin term, 'clap of thunder'.

FLICKER *n.* 19th century. A measure of alcohol, specifically a glass.

FLIP *n.* 17th century. A drink of small beer and brandy, mixed together and heated.

"FORTY-ROD LIGHTNING" *n.* 19th century. Strong but cheap whisky.

FORTY-ROD LIGHTNING *n.* 19th century. Strong but cheap whisky.

TO BE FOXED *v.* 17th century. To be drunk. Compares being drunk with being confused. 'To fox' is also to make drunk.

FRENCH ELIXIR *n.* 19th century. Brandy. From its origins in France, and the fact that it was viewed as having medicinal properties.

FULLER'S EARTH *n.* 19th century. Gin. For the way it acts to clean out or scour a person's insides.

GAY AND FRISKY *n.* 19th century. Rhyming slang for 'whisky'.

TO GET THE GRAVEL RASH *v.* 19th century. To be drunk to the point of falling over, therefore to be injured by the pavement (gravel).

GIN LANE *n.* 19th century. Alimentary thoroughfare which receives heavy booze traffic, i.e. the mouth of a drunkard.

TO GIVE THE BOTTLE A BLACK EYE *v.* 18th century. To drink alcohol, especially to drink excessively or get drunk. A predecessor to the modern term 'hit the bottle'.

GRAPPLE THE RAILS *n.* 18th century. Whisky. Named for the physical effect drinking it would have on the drinker, making them need to grab on to the rails to stay standing.

GROG *n*. 19th century. A naval term, meaning a mixture of rum and water, which became synonymous with alcoholic drinks in general. Still in use.

GROG-SHOP *n*. 19th century. Mouth, after its function in welcoming the consumption of alcoholic beverages. Also a play on the common name for a public house.

HAIR OF THE DOG *n*. In constant use since the 16th century, this term for a hangover cure of another drink, or 'hair of the dog that bit you' stems from the superstition that burning the hair of a dog would act as a cure for its bite.

HALF AND HALF *n.* 18th century. A mix of ale and beer. Similar to 'snakebite', which is a mix of beer and cider.

HEAVY WET *n.* 19th century. Beer, particularly porter or stout. 'Wet' here means an alcoholic drink, and 'heavy' refers to beer's deep colour and thick consistency. The phrase 'a pint of heavy', meaning a pint of stout, is still used in Scottish pubs. See also LIGHT WET.

HUCKLE MY BUTT *n.* 18th/19th century. A drink of brandy mixed with egg and heated.

HUMMING BUB *n.* 19th century. Strong beer, 'bub' meaning drink, and the 'humming' most likely refers to the sensation one would get, especially in the head, when drinking strong beer.

TO IRRIGATE ONE'S TONSILS *v.* 18th century. To lavish one's throat with groggy affection, i.e. to drink, especially an alcoholic drink. Also seen as 'to irrigate one's canal'. Tonsils and canal both refer to the throat, and the irrigation suggests pouring liquid down the throat.

JIGGER STUFF *n.* 19th century. A secret still. 'Jigger' here means a key, so the still would be locked-up, away from prying eyes. 'Jigger' therefore meant illegal or bootleg alcohol.

TO BE JUG-BITTEN *v.* 17th century. To receive an intoxicating nip from the ale flagon; to be drunk.

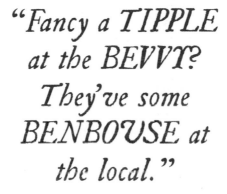

"*Fancy a TIPPLE at the BEVVY? They've some BENBOUSE at the local.*"

TIPPLE – An alcoholic drink
BEVVY – Pub
BENBOUSE – Good quality beer

"JIGGER STUFF"
n. 19th century.
Bootleg alcohol.

KNOCK DOWN *n.* 19th century. Beer. Also seen 'knock me down'. For the effects of drinking beer, especially in large quantities.

LAP *n.* 16th century. A drink of any variety. Comes from the idea of 'lapping up' a liquid.

TO BE LAPPING THE GUTTER *v.* 19th century. To be drunk to the point of having fallen over, therefore to have one's face in the gutter, which will likely be full of water.

LIGHT WET *n.* 19th century. Gin. 'Wet' was used to refer to an alcoholic drink, and 'light' is used for gin due to its colourlessness and thin consistency. See also HEAVY WET.

LIVENER *n.* 19th century. The first alcoholic drink of the day. Particularly for a seasoned drinker or alcoholic, this would have an 'enlivening' effect.

TO LUSH IT UP *v.* 19th century. To drink an excessive amount of alcohol. 'To lush it around' is also used in the same context, and a lush is a drunk or an alcoholic, which is still in common usage.

TO MAKE A PEARL ON THE NAIL *v.*
17th century. To drink (alcohol) down to the
last drop. The term is derived from a 16th-
century practice, where the last drop of a
drink was poured onto the left thumbnail.

MERRY-GO-DOWN   *n.*   18th/19th
century. A drink of strong ale which
had been heated. A play on the popular
fairground merry-go-round, named for
the idea that the drink would go down
easily, and make the drinker merry.

TO BE ALL MOPS AND BROOMS *v.* 19th
century. To be drunk. From *mop*, a drinking
bout or a drunk.

MOTHER'S BLESSING *n*. 19th century. Laudanum, which is a mixture of brandy and opium. Thus called because it was often given to children to keep them quiet or make them sleep, therefore making their mothers feel 'blessed' with some quiet time.

MOTHER'S MILK *n*. 19th century. Gin. Suggests a love for the drink, to the point of addiction. Also references that many gin drinkers were women. Linked to the modern term 'mother's ruin', which puts gin, less subtly, into a negative light.

MUZZLER *n*. 19th century. A measure of alcohol, derived from 'muzzle', meaning mouth. It most likely simply meant a mouthful.

NANTZ *n.* 19th century. Brandy, from the French town of Nantes, a hub for Cognac production. Seen also as 'cold nantz'.

NECTAR *n.* 19th century. An alcoholic drink, especially a particularly enjoyable one.

NIPPITATUM *n.* 18th century. Beer, or any other strong alcoholic drink. Seen also as 'nippitato' and 'nippitate'.

OLD MAN'S MILK *n.* 19th century. Whisky. Related to *mother's milk*, gin. Suggests that while women would predominantly turn to gin to drown their sorrows, old men would turn to whisky.

TO BE OUT OF REGISTER *v.* 19th century. To be drunk, and stumbling around. From a printers' term meaning badly set type.

PEG *n.* 19th century. A measure of alcohol. Described by the Oxford English Dictionary as 'one of a set of pins fixed at intervals in a drinking vessel as marks to measure the quantity which each drinker was to drink'.

PICKLED *adj.* 18th century. To attempt to preserve one's liver, kidneys, etc. in alcohol by consuming as much as possible, i.e. to be drunk.

"NIPPITATUM"
n. 18th century. Beer
or other alcohol.

POISON *n*. 19th century. Health-threatening but ultimately satisfying alcoholic beverage of any sort. Seen especially in the phrase 'What's your poison?' meaning what would you like to drink. Still in common usage.

PONGELOW *n*. 19th century. Beer. Used by the Indian Army, 'pong' meaning to drink. Seen also as 'ponjello'.

TO PRIME YOURSELF *v*. 19th century. To pluck up some Dutch courage; to ply oneself with (excessive amounts) of alcohol.

REDEYE *n.* 19th century. Whisky, for the way drinking it would turn the whites of the eyes red and bloodshot. See also WHITE EYE.

REPOSER *n.* 19th century. An evening tipple; a nightcap.

ROTGUT *n.* 16th century. Ale which rots the guts of those who consume it.

ROYAL POVERTY *n.* 18th century. Gin. From the fact that many of the queen's subjects would drink themselves into poverty on gin, and that many of the poor tried to improve their daily lot with the consumption of gin.

"SLUMGULLION"
n. 19th century.
An unpleasant alcoholic drink.

SALISBURY *n.* 17th century. A gallon pot with a tap, used for wine.

SEEING THE DEVIL *v.* 18th century. To be drunk, the devil being the drink.

SLUMGULLION *n.* 19th century. An unpleasant alcoholic drink, one which would only be drunk as a last resort. Also refers to fish offal, which explains how disgusting the drink in question would be considered.

TO SOAK THE CLAY *v.* 19th century. To nourish the dust (mortal clay) that constitutes man and woman with alcoholic liquid.

TO BE SOZZLED *v.* 19th century. To be drunk. From 'sozzly' meaning sloppy, or 'sozzle' meaning 'to moisten'. Still in common usage.

TO SPLICE THE MAIN BRACE *v.* A nautical term, this was one of the most difficult and dangerous tasks to perform on a ship, so whoever did the job would receive an extra ration of rum. The phrase has been in use since the 16th century, and became synonymous with drinking due to its link to rum rations.

TO STAB ONESELF AND PASS THE DAGGER *v.* 19th century. To take a drink and pass the bottle round. A theatrical term.

STINGO *n.* 17th century. Beer, for the way it 'stings' when drunk.

STRIP-ME-NAKED *n.* 19th century. Raw gin, for what it would do to your insides when you drank it.

TO SUCK THE MONKEY *v.* 18th century. Despite sounding quite crude, this naval term means to drink alcohol through a straw. Also seen as 'to tap the admiral'.

SWANKEY *n.* 19th century. Beer, specifically the best beer. From 'swanky', meaning pretentious.

SWIZZLE *n*. 19th century. An alcoholic drink, one that will make someone intoxicated. Still used in the context of a 'swizzle stick', which is used for mixing up a mixed drink or cocktail.

TANGLE-LEG *n*. 19th century. Gin. From the effect drinking gin would have on a person's coordination.

TIPPER *n*. 19th century. A type of ale, named for the Brighton brewer Thomas Tipper. It was brewed from brackish water from one particular well.

TIPPLE *n*. 16th century. A wee drop of something alcoholic. Still in common usage, particularly to mean a little drink.

WET *adj.* 16th century. Drunk, from the liquid nature of alcohol.

TO WET ONE'S WHISTLE *v.* 14th century. To drink (alcohol). From 'whistle', meaning throat, which you wet with the drink of choice. Used by Chaucer. Still in use.

WHITE EYE *n.* 19th century. Whisky. From the way a person's eyes could roll back into their head, exposing the whites, if they had drunk too much.

WIBBLE *n.* 18th century. Gin. Likely from the way consumption makes a person feel. Can also be used as a word for any weak alcoholic drink.

INTIMATE
RELATIONS

LOVE and MARRIAGE
Or relations between Gaffers, Gammers, Back-door men and Freelances

BACK-DOOR MAN *n.* 19th century. An adulterous man. One who would sneak in via the back door to see his paramour without being seen. Not to be confused with a GENTLEMAN OF THE BACK DOOR.

BENE MORT *n.* 16th century. A pretty girl, or a good girl, 'bene' meaning good.

BILLY-NOODLE *n.* 19th century. A man who believes himself to be irresistible to the opposite sex, despite evidence to the contrary. From the US.

DUCK *n*. 16th century. Lover. Used with this meaning by the Old Bard himself. Still in common usage, particularly in the north or England, though usually used interchangeably with 'luv' as a friendly gesture, rather than to denote a lover.

FLAME *n*. 19th century. Inamorato. From the French *flame*, which was popular in romantic novels. Especially used as 'old flame', meaning ex-lover, and this meaning is still in use today. 'Flame' can also, somewhat ironically, be used to mean sexually transmitted disease, likely from the burning sensation many such diseases would cause.

FREELANCE *n*. 19th century. An adulterous woman, one with many partners, but not a whore. The suggested freedom here is shared with the male equivalent, *freeman*, and 'lance' is quite likely a play on the penis' shape.

FREEMAN *n*. 18th century. A man who is free and easy with his affections, i.e. an adulterer.

GAFFER *n*. 18th century. Husband. This term is still in use today, but more often to describe a foreman or supervisor.

GAMMER *n*. 18th century. Wife. Female equivalent of a GAFFER.

LEFT-HANDED WIFE *n.* 19th century. A mistress. Being 'left-handed' or 'sinister' shows the relationship to be suspect; the woman in question is a 'wife' only in the bedroom.

LOTEBY *n.* 14th century. A paramour. From the standard English word 'lote', meaning to hide or skulk, as this is what mistresses invariably had to do. Also seen as 'ludby'.

"FREEMAN"
n. 18th century. An adulterer.

LOTHARIO *n.* 17th century. A male debaucher or dallier. From the name given to the 'young gallant' in Sir William Davenant's 1627 play, *The Cruel Brother*.

MISS *n.* 17th century. A mistress. Ironic, as 'miss' suggests someone virginal, which such a woman would not be. Also likely an abbreviation of mistress.

PETTICOAT GOVERNMENT *n.* 17th century. A home in which the wife holds the power.

PETTICOAT LED *adj.* 17th century. A man infatuated, possibly to the point of being 'under the thumb'.

PINTLE-FANCIER *n.* 19th century. A promiscuous girl.

PURE *n.* 17th century. A mistress. An ironic term, suggesting such a woman was actually the exact opposite. See also MISS.

RUM BLOWEN *n.* 18th century. A good-looking, handsome woman, 'rum' meaning good, 'blowen' woman.

SHE-FAMILIAR *n.* 19th century. A moll; a bed-mate; a mistress. Shows the intimacy of the relationship, and also has sinister overtones, alluding to a witch's familiar.

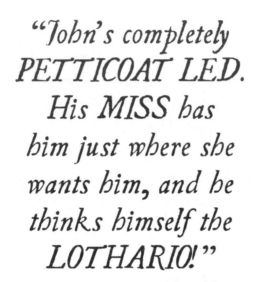

"John's completely *PETTICOAT LED*. His *MISS* has him just where she wants him, and he thinks himself the *LOTHARIO!*"

PETTICOAT LED – Infatuated
MISS – Mistress
LOTHARIO – Male debaucher

WEEKENDER *n.* 19th century. A ladylove who is only available for consultation on Saturdays and Sundays.

WITTOL *n.* 15th century. A complacent husband, whose wife is being adulterous, and who makes no effort to change this. From the standard English name for a variety of bird which is often prey to the cuckoo, the woodwale. This bird ends up raising the cuckoo's young in place of its own, just as a husband who is a 'wittol' would likely end up raising another man's child.

SEX
Or the ins and outs of
Firkytoodle and Leg Business

TO ACCOMODATE *v.* 19th century. To copulate. From 'accommodation house', a brothel. Likely because the girls therein were so obliging.

APHRODISIACAL TENNIS COURT *n.* A place where one can work up a sweat by batting around a few balls; a lady's love playground, i.e. the vagina. 17th century. A euphemism used by Sir Thomas Urquhart, the first man to translate Rabelais.

ATHANASIAN WENCH *n.* 18th/19th century. A girl happy to go with any man who asks her, an 'easy' girl.

BALLOCKS *n, pl*. Testicles. In use since the 11th century, this was originally standard English. In modern usage this term is usually spelt 'bollocks'.

BATH OF BIRTH *n*. 19th century. The dewy cradle of newborn babies, i.e. the vagina. Euphemism used by American poet Walt Whitman.

BEARD *n*. 17th/18th century. Female pubic hair. Still in use, especially as 'bearded...' for descriptions of the vagina.

BEARD-JAMMER *n*. 17th century. The fleshy instrument used to investigate a lady's hirsute nether regions, i.e. a penis. Also a promiscuous man. Seen also as BEARD SPLITTER.

"BLUBBER"
n. 18th century.
Breasts.

BELLE-CHOSE *n.* 14th century. A lady's private area. A positive euphemism from the French, meaning beautiful thing. Term used by Chaucer.

TO GET A BELLY-BUMPER *v.* 19th century. To become pregnant.

BEST LEG OF THREE *n.* 19th century. The tallywhacker. The 'third leg' idea is still prevalent today, and the 'best' part of this name is likely due to the more pleasurable nature of this 'third leg'.

BEST PART *n.* 16th/17th century. Vagina. A positive euphemism, employed by John Donne. See also WORST PART.

BLUBBER *n.* 18th century. Breasts, after their fattiness. Also used to mean the mouth.

BRAT-GETTER *n.* 19th century. A man's procreative part.

BUBBIES *n, pl.* 17th century. Breasts. Along with 'bubs', developed into the modern terms 'boobs' and 'boobies'.

BUGGER *n.* 16th century. A man who practices sodomy, a sodomite.

BUM-RANGER *n.* 18th century. Penis. Bum not necessarily referring to the anus but to the sexual organs in general, therefore, tool for ranging this area. Also a promiscuous man.

BUSH *n.* Pubic hair, either male or female, but predominantly used for female. In continuous use since the 19th century.

BUTTERED BUN *n.* A woman who has had intercourse with a number of men in quick succession, most likely for how moist her 'bun' would be after large amounts of intercourse. Modern usage stems from the 17th century, though the term was first coined in the 16th century for the courtesan Louise de Quérouaille.

CATERWAUL *n.* 16th century. Originally meaning the noise made by mating cats, this came to mean foreplay, suggesting not only noise, but also the mutual stimulation which would cause such noise.

CAVAULT *v.* 17th century. To copulate, for the energetic and pleasurable nature of the sexual act.

CHAUVERER *n.* 19th century. Promiscuous man. From 'chauver', meaning 'to have sex'.

CHERRY *n.* 19th century. A virgin. Was used to denote a female virgin, but modern usage, e.g. 'pop your cherry' (lose your virginity) is applied to both male and female. Links with 'cherry ripe': 'She is cherry ripe, and ready for the picking'.

CLAPTRAP *n.* 18th century. Vagina. From a theatrical term which meant using gags and tricks to get applause, in this sense it was suggestive that the vagina was a trap for the 'clap' – sexually transmitted diseases. Still in common use, but now with the meaning of nonsense, or talking rubbish, e.g. 'Don't talk such claptrap'. 'The clap' is still used as a term for venereal disease.

COCK *n.* Dong; dick; dangler. In constant use since the 15th century, but was considered standard English until the 18th century. Directly compares the shape of the penis to a cockerel's head.

COCK BAWD *n.* 18th/19th century. A male brothel owner, 'cock' representing his masculinity, being both a male chicken and slang for the penis, and 'bawd' referring to a bawdy house or brothel. Also sometimes used to mean pimp, or indeed male prostitute, and can denote a small firelighter, as it brings the fire to the coals, the way a brothel owner lights the fires of their customers.

COCKISH *adj.* 16th century. Originally meant essentially the same as 'cocky', one who uses bravado and has a high opinion of themselves. However, by the 18th century, when the word appeared in Grose's *The Vulgar Tongue*, it had come to mean wanton or forward.

CORNUCOPIA *n.* 19th century. Vagina. A cornucopia is a horn of plenty, therefore linking the vagina both to food, and suggesting it is the source of all good things.

COVENT GARDEN NUN *n.* 18th century. A prostitute. A play on Covent Garden being a hotspot for prostitution, and its origins as the home of a convent.

CRANNY *n.* 19th century. A lady's 'nook', i.e. vagina. After the vagina as a corner or slit. See also CRANNY-HUNTER.

CRANNY-HUNTER *n.* 19th century. A fleshy implement use to beat around a woman's bush, i.e. a cock.

CULLS *n.* 17th century. Testicles. From the Latin *coleus* meaning 'a strainer bag'.

CUNDUM *n.* 18th/19th century. A sheath made of dried sheep's guts, worn by a man during intercourse to prevent venereal disease, purported to have been invented by a Colonel Cundum, though he may be a fictional character.

"CRANNY"
n. 19th century. A vagina.

CUNT *n.* fanny; quim. Also used as an insult, especially for a woman. In common usage since the 13th century, when it was mentioned in the Oxford English Dictionary with reference to *Gropecuntelane*, a street in Southwark which formed part of the brothel area. By the 16th century it was considered highly vulgar, and by the 19th, the word had been banned as legally obscene. Many other slang terms have spawned from this one word, though none have outlasted it.

CUNT-CURTAIN *n.* 19th century. Luxuriously hairy draping framing the vulva.

CUPID'S FURROW *n.* 18th/19th century. Vagina. Used by poet Robert Burns in his collection, *The Merry Muses of Caledonia*. This work was more bawdy than his usual poetry and contained several euphemisms for the vagina.

DAIRY *n*. 18th/19th century. A woman's breasts, particularly a nursing mother, for their ability to produce milk.

TO DO A BIT OF FRONT-DOOR WORK *v*. 19th century. To work up a sweat labouring at a lady's main entrance, i.e. to have sex, 'front door' referring to the vagina, the opposite of the 'back door', the anus.

TO DOCK *v*. 18th/19th century. Seafaring phrase meaning to successfully manoeuvre one's 'barge' into a vacant 'mooring spot', i.e. to have sex with a woman, often a prostitute.

"DOXIES"
n, pl. 16th century.
Female beggars.

TO DO SOMEONE *v.* 16th century. To have sex with someone. One of the most enduring terms for sexual activity, still in common usage. Used by the Old Bard himself, e.g. 'I have done thy mother' in *Titus Andronicus.*

DOWNSHIRE *n.* 19th century. A minor hillock with a light covering of down, i.e. a lady's muff. Can also be used for the vagina.

DOXIES *n, pl.* 16th century. Prostitutes or female beggars. Possibly stems from the Middle Dutch word *docke*, which means doll.

EEL-POT *n.* 19th century. Vagina. Final destination for a man's wriggling, trouser pet. Term suggests the female genitals' use as a receptacle, the eel being the penis.

EYE THAT WEEPS MOST WHEN BEST PLEASED *n.* 18th century. The honey pot; the cunny, the vagina. Lengthy euphemism used by playwright and actor G. A. Stevens.

FANNY *n.* 19th century. Vagina. Many link this term with John Cleland's 1748 novel, *Memoirs of a Woman of Pleasure*, which was, and is, known popularly by its heroine's name, *Fanny Hill*. Still in common usage.

TO FEEL ONE'S WAY TO HEAVEN *v.* 18th century. To take part in foreplay, to stimulate someone with the hand. 'Heaven' here may refer to orgasm, or to the pubic region itself.

FIRESHIP *n.* 17th century. A prostitute with sexually transmitted infections. If a man 'boards' her, he will burn with the fire of venereal disease afterwards. The male equivalent is a 'fireplug'.

FIRKYTOODLE *n.* 17th century. Foreplay. Means 'to play with'. 'Firk' on its own means 'to beat', which is, again, associated with sex.

FISH *n.* 17th century. A bawd; also a lady's lower regions. Possibly attributable to the perceived smell of an unwashed woman's vagina, a description which is still used in offensive language.

FISHMONGER *n.* 17th century. He who buys 'fish' (bawds) for sale at the 'market'. Referring both to the 'fish' he buys, and to the amount of vaginas he has bought into.

TO FIST A MAN *v.* 17th century. To masturbate a man. Used by The Old Bard in *Henry IV, Part Two*, when Fang says to Mistress Quickly 'If I but fist him once, if he come but within my vice.' This double-entendre can be read as a threat, 'If I punch him, if he comes close to my grip', or as having sexual overtones, 'If I masturbate him, if he were to come in my hand.'

FLAPDOODLE *n.* 17th century. The flipping, flapping, flaccid male member.

FLAT-COCK *n.* 17th century. Woman. Sexual description based on the female genitalia, especially the clitoris.

FLOWER OF CHIVALRY *n.* 19th century. Vagina. Puns on chivalry, which is riding, therefore referencing the act of copulation. See also LADY FLOWER.

FOIN *v.* 14th century. To fuck; to fornicate. From the standard English term, which means 'to thrust with a weapon, especially a pointed one'.

FOOL TRAP *n.* 19th century. Vagina. Reminiscent of a fly-trap, this suggests only a fool is taken in by a woman and her sexual wiles. Possibly also a reference to being fooled into marriage after sleeping with a woman.

FOREBUTTOCKS *n*, *pl*. 18th century. A lady's chest-bum; the breasts. After their rounded appearance, like buttocks, especially when lifted by corsetry. Originally coined by the poet Alexander Pope around 1727.

FOUTRE *v*. 16th century. Fuck, used as an expletive, not necessarily as a term for sex. From the French, this term can also be spelt 'foutra', which underlines the English-speaker's way of emphasising French pronunciation.

"FOIN"
v. 14th century. To fornicate.

THE FRAIL SISTERHOOD *n*, *pl*. 19th Century. Prostitutes, usually higher-class ones.

FRIG *v*. 18th century. Fuck, as an expletive, such as 'Oh, frig!' Also seen in 'frigging', which is used in the same way as 'fucking', e.g. 'frigging hell'. Frigging's other meaning is masturbation.

FUCK *v*. 16th century. To have sex. Standard English until the 17th century, when it started to be considered slang and vulgar, which it has remained. It first appeared in a dictionary in 1598, in John Florio's *Worlde of Wordes*, which defined '*Fottere*, to iape, to sard, to fucke, to swive, to occupy.' One of the most enduring slang terms, it is used not only to denote sexual intercourse, but also as an expletive.

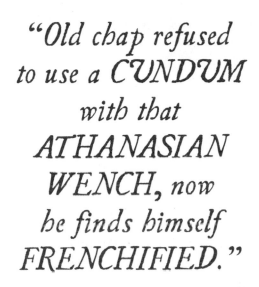

"Old chap refused to use a CUNDUM with that ATHANASIAN WENCH, now he finds himself FRENCHIFIED."

CUNDUM – Condom
ATHANASIAN WENCH – Trollop
FRENCHIFIED – Infected with venereal disease

"FUMBLE"
n. 16th century.
Foreplay.

FUCKSTER *n.* 19th century. A man who has sex often, with reference to the ubiquitous FUCK.

FUMBLE *n.* 16th century. Foreplay, particularly when inexperienced/in the dark. Still in use.

GAPSTOPPER *n.* 18th century. A wedge to bridge a lady's gap, a penis. After the act of penetration. Also a promiscuous man.

GENTLEMAN OF THE BACK DOOR *n.* 18th century. A homosexual man, or sodomite. 'Back door' here equates to the anus. Using 'back door' as a term for anus is still common.

GILFLURT *n.* 18th/19th century. A vain woman or minx. Related to the verb 'to flirt'.

TO GIVE A GREEN GOWN *v.* 19th century. To indulge in some outdoor activities of the procreative kind – specifically, to have sex on the grass and thus acquire a 'green gown' from all the rolling and tumbling. Has implications of deflowering, losing virginity.

TO DO THE GOAT'S JIG *v.* Also seen as 'to dance the goat's jig'. To have sex. Described by Grose as 'old', this term dates from before the 18th century. The 'jig' refers to sex as a dance between two people, and 'goat' here refers to the devil, sex being seen as 'the devil's work'.

GOBBLE-PRICK *n.* 18th century. A woman who is hungry for a filling; a lusty woman who enjoys sex, after both the act of penetration and fellatio.

GROPING FOR TROUTS IN A PECULIAR RIVER *v.* 17th century. To copulate. Coined by Old Bill himself in *Measure for Measure*.

TO HAVE A BIT OF GIBLET PIE *v.* 18th century. To do the nasty; to have sex. References the genitals, 'giblets' being a man's penis and testicles, and 'pie' being the vagina. Explicitly suggests encasing the penis in the vagina.

TO HAVE SOMEONE *v.* 16th century. To copulate with someone. Like 'do', 'have' is one of the most enduring terms for sex and is still in circulation. Shakespeare used it in *Richard III*: 'I'll have her – but I will not keep her long.'

TO BE HIT ON THE MASTER VEIN *v.* 16th century. To conceive; to be made pregnant. See also MASTERPIECE.

HIVE *n.* 17th century. The honeypot; the cranny. Also seen as 'beehive'. A place full of honey, which can mean either partner's sexual fluids. Still in use.

HONEYPOT *n.* 17th century. Vagina. Like HIVE, suggests a place full of honey (sexual fluids). Became more popular again in the mid-20th century due to 1958's *Candy* by Terry Southern. Still in use.

HUMP *v.* 18th century. To bump uglies; to bury the weasel, i.e. to have sex . Likely from the shape made by the two people's backs when they are in the act, hunched together. Still in common usage, though often meaning to rub against someone without actually using penetration.

INDORSER *n.* 16th century. An alternate spelling of 'endorser' which, according to Grose's *The Vulgar Tongue*, is also used to denote a man who practices sodomy, probably due to the word's roots in the French term *endosser*, meaning 'to put on the back'.

TO GET JACK IN THE ORCHARD *v.* 19th century. To have sex. The orchard here refers to the vagina.

JELLY *n.* 19th century. A pretty girl with large breasts.

JELLY-BAG *n.* 17th century. Balls; goolies; gonads. Likely named for the consistency of the testicles. This term is also sometimes used to mean vagina.

JOHN AMONG THE MAIDS *n.* 19th century. A stud; a man who is popular with the ladies, sexually.

KEYHOLE *n.* 19th century. The place a man may insert his veiny lock-pick, i.e. the quim.

TO KNOCK *v.* 16th century. To have sexual intercourse. The term 'knocking shop', meaning brothel, is still used today.

"JELLY BAG"
n. 17th century.
Balls; goolies; gonads.

LACED MUTTON *n*. A prostitute. Likely 16th century, along with *mutton* and *mutton-monger*. From *mutton* meaning vagina or woman, particularly a prostitute, and 'laced' suggesting corsetry, so as to provide a more attractively shaped woman.

LADIES' TAILOR *n*. 19th century. A promiscuous man, after the in and out motion of both sewing and the physical act of intercourse.

LADY FLOWER *n*. 19th century. A pink-petalled posy growing on Downshire, i.e. the vagina. Euphemism used by the American poet Walt Whitman. Describing the vagina in terms of a flower has continued on, with the modern term 'lady garden' most likely being directly related.

LEATHERSTRETCHER *n.* 18th century. A tool for loosening the horse-collar, i.e. the penis. Leather being a term for the vagina, which the penis would stretch during sex. Also a promiscuous man.

LEG BUSINESS *n.* 19th century. The act of getting one's 'leg over', i.e. sexual intercourse.

LEGLIFTER *n.* 18th century. A man with a large sexual appetite.

TO LIFT THE HEELS *v.* 19th century. To have sexual intercourse.

"Just off to see the local DOXY about some LEG BUSINESS. Let's hope I don't come back with a PINTLE-FEVER like last time!"

DOXY – Prostitute
LEG BUSINESS – Sexual intercourse
PINTLE-FEVER – Venereal disease

LOVE-APPLES *n.* 19th century. Hanging fruit which grows at the base of the veiny love tree, i.e. the testicles. After their shape, and their purpose in intercourse/procreation.

LOVE-DART *n.* 18th century. Cock; knob; penis. Refers both to the penis' part in the act of copulation, and to it being a weapon, or tool.

LOVE-LANE *n.* 19th century. A place where John Thomas may skip happily along, i.e. the vagina. After the act of making love.

LOWER-WIG *n.* 19th century. The hair down there, i.e. pubic hair (usually female). As wigs were still commonly worn, referring to this hair as a wig made sense.

"MINGE"
n. 19th century.
Vagina.

LUSTY-GUTS *n.* 16th century. A man with a large sexual appetite.

TO MAKE THE BEAST WITH TWO BACKS *v.* To have sex, for the way two people look like when joined together, during the act. Used by Shakespeare in *Othello*.

MARRIAGE GEAR *n.* 18th century. Consummation equipment, i.e. the tallywhacker. For the fact that sex is meant to take place after marriage, especially on the wedding night. See also WEDDING TACKLE.

MASTERPIECE *n.* 18th century. A 'private' work of art; a vagina. See also TO BE HIT ON THE MASTER VEIN.

MELL *v.* 14th century. To have sex. A euphemistic term, which comes from the standard English meaning to mix or to blend.

MERRYMAKER *n.* 19th century. The giggle-stick, i.e. the penis. After its purpose in sexual intercourse, thereby making both partners 'merry'.

MINGE *n.* 19th century. Vagina. Suffolk dialect, originally from old Romany. Still in common usage.

MOLLY *n.* 18th century. A homosexual man. Suggests feminine traits. Also developed into 'moll-house', a gay men's meeting-house.

THE MONOSYLLABLE *n.* 18th century. Fanny. A euphemism for the monosyllabic term CUNT. First written down in *The Vulgar Tongue* by Frances Grose.

MOUTH THAT CANNOT BITE *n.* 17th century. Vagina. Euphemism which plays on the vagina as an opening. Employed by the playwright Thomas D'Urfey (sometimes spelt Durfey).

MUFF *n.* 17th century. Female pubic hair. Also used to mean vagina. Still in common usage with both meanings. See entry in Everyday Words and Phrases: People for alternate meaning.

NATURE'S DUTY *n.* 19th century. The sexual act. Likely related to *nature* as a term for penis, so it is not just a person's natural duty to procreate, but also the duty of the penis specifically.

NATURE'S FOUNTS *n*, *pl*. 19th century. Soft, fleshy protrusions from which springs a nourishing elixir, i.e. breasts. After the breasts' milk-producing capacity.

NAUGHTY *n*. 19th century. Vagina. Probably stemming from the idea that the vagina itself was a cause of naughtiness. Still in use in the form 'naughty bits'.

TO DO THE NAUGHTY *v*. 19th century. To have sexual intercourse. Likely related to the use of NAUGHTY as a slang term for vagina. Still in use.

NEEDLEWOMAN *n*. 19th century. Prostitute. After 'needle', being the penis. Likely also referencing the in-out motion of both sewing and sexual intercourse. See also LADIES' TAILOR.

NETHER LIPS *n.* 14th century. Vagina. A euphemism referring to the vaginal lips and their location, low on the body. Term used by Chaucer.

NIMROD *n.* 18th century. Penis. Both after the 'mighty hunter' who appears in *Genesis*, and as a pun on 'rod'.

NUGGING HOUSE *n.* 17th century. A brothel, a place where people go to NUG.

TO NUG *v.* 17th century. To have sex with someone. From the term NUGGING HOUSE, meaning brothel.

OLD HORNINGTON *n.* 18th century. Penis. A literal name for the penis, along the lines of the eternally popular 'John Thomas'.

PECULIAR *n.* A mistress. From the standard English word which entered the language around the 15th century, meaning 'exclusive to one person'. Suggests that the mistress belongs to her paramour.

PECULIAR RIVER *n.* 17th century. A place where trouser-eels frolic, i.e. the vagina. Coined by the Dusty Old Playwright himself in *Measure for Measure*.

"*PECULIAR*"
n. A mistress.

PENWIPER *n.* 19th century. A part for de-clogging one's nib, i.e. the fanny. Referencing the sexual act; pen being the penis, wiping being the movement.

PETTICOAT MERCHANT *n.* 17th century. A whoremonger; one whose business is in petticoats.

PETTISH *adj.* 17th century. Immodest or passionate, particularly in a woman. In use since the 16th century, but its earlier use meant insolent, without the sexual overtone.

PIECE OF STUFF *n.* A sexually attractive woman, a woman as a sexual commodity. Continuation of the use of *piece* as a term for a woman, 17th century, still in use.

PINTLE *n.* Penis. From the Anglo-Saxon 'pintel' and standard English from the 12th to the 18th century. Gave rise to several related slang terms.

PINTLE-FEVER *n.* 18th/19th century. Venereal disease. Literally fever of the penis.

PINTLE-MERCHANT *n.* 19th century. She who deals in pintle (penis), i.e. a prostitute.

PITCHER *n.* 17th century. The cup that runneth over with seed; the furry cup; the vagina. Sees the female genitals as a literal receptacle (for the penis or semen).

PIZZLE *n*. 16th century. A gentleman's 'main vein'; the cock. Prior to the mid-16th century, this term was used to denote an animal's penis, but then became slang for the human penis. Likely from 'piss', referencing the penis' primary function.

PLOVER *n*. 17th century. Prostitute. Went on to become a general (derogatory) term for a woman in the 19th century. Describes a woman as a 'bird'. Seen also as 'pheasant' and 'quail'.

POONTS *n, pl*. 19th century. Breasts. Named after fonts.

POOR MAN'S BLESSING *n.* 19th century. Vagina. Likely suggests that sex is the only place a poor man will be able to find happiness and satisfaction, as he lacks in material goods.

PRIVATES *n.* 19th century. Penis. A classic evasion of naming the penis. Still in common usage, though now the phrase is used for both male and female genitals.

PUSSY *n.* 17th century. Woman, specifically as a sex object. Also, later became a word for the vagina, the latter definition is still in common usage.

TO PUT THE DEVIL INTO HELL *v.* 19th century. To have sex, the 'devil' being the penis, and 'hell' being the vagina.

QUIM *n.* 18th century. Vagina. Still widely used.

QUIM WHISKERS *n.* 18th century. Female pubic hair. QUIM being the vagina, and whiskers being related to the whiskers on a man's face. This is likely related to BEARD, as well as CUNT-CURTAIN.

"George met a *PETTISH GILFLURT* at the *NUGGING HOUSE*, maybe she'll be his *PECULIAR*."

PETTISH – Passionate
GILFLURT – Minx
NUGGING HOUSE – Brothel
PECULIAR – Mistress

"SCRUB"
n. 18th century.
A cheap prostitute.

RENTER *n.* 19th century. A male prostitute. Developed into the modern phrase 'rent boy'.

SCREW *v.* 18th century. To have sex. The first term which compares sex to a DIY task, and one of the most enduring slang terms for sex.

SCRUB *n.* 18th century. A cheap prostitute.

SEMINARY *n.* 19th century. A seed plot, i.e. fanny. A punning name, referencing the vagina as a receptacle for semen.

SHAG *v.* 14th century. To secrete the sausage; to butter the gherkin; to bonk. In standard English, it means 'to shake'. Still in common usage, also as a noun, 'a shag' meaning a sexual encounter, or someone a person has had sex with.

SILENT BEARD *n.* 19th century. Hairy adornment of a mouth which cannot speak, i.e. female pubic hair.

SNATCH *n.* 19th century. Vagina. Suggests a vicious or violent nature to the female genitals. Still in common usage.

SPLIT-ARSE MECHANIC *n.* 18th/19th century. A prostitute. A play on her profession, therefore 'mechanic'. 'Split-arse' likely refers to the fact that many prostitutes used anal penetration as a way of avoiding pregnancy.

TO STAB *v.* 16th century. To have sex with, specifically the act of a man penetrating someone. Compares the penis to a weapon. One of Old Bill himself's preferred terms for sex. Seen also as 'to stab someone in the thigh'.

STAFF BREAKER *n.* 19th century. She who has the power to render a man's baton useless, i.e. a sexually promiscuous woman, who copulates with gusto. See STAFF OF LIFE.

STAFF CLIMBER *n.* 19th century. A woman with a strong sexual appetite. See STAFF OF LIFE.

STAFF OF LIFE *n.* 19th century. The rod of power; the magic wand, i.e. the cock. From the shape and the role played in reproduction.

SWIVE *v.* 15th century. To have sex. Started as a literary, standard English term, but became slang, and considered vulgar, in the 17th century, at the same times as the terms FUCK and *sard*.

TALLYWHACKER *n.* 18th century. Penis. Relating to 'tally', a type of notched stick.

TICKLE THOMAS *n.* 19th century. Vagina. Referencing the sexual act, Thomas being the penis.

TO TIP THE VELVET *v.* 19th century. To perform cunnilingus, after the use of the tip of the tongue. A phrase made famous more recently by the Sarah Waters book, *Tipping the Velvet*, and the BBC adaptation of the same name.

TITS *n.* 19th century. Breasts. From teats, meaning nipples, but used to reference the whole breast. Still in common use.

TOOL *n.* Penis. From the Old Norse *tol*, which means to make or to prepare. In constant use since the 13th century, an enduring slang term equating the penis with the fact it has a specific purpose. In modern usage, often employed as an insult along the lines of 'idiot'.

TOTTY *n.* 19th century. A nice bit of stuff; a high-class prostitute. Still in usage but with the toned-down meaning of a sexually attractive woman.

TOWN BULL *n.* 17th century. The local expert quim-basher, i.e. the most promiscuous man in the town, the man with the reputation for bedding the most women.

TREASURE OF LOVE *n.* 18th century. A lady's jewellery box, i.e. vagina. Used by John Cleland in *Memoirs of a Woman of Pleasure*, his 1749 erotic novel. Cleland avoided the use of obscenity with several such words.

TO TUP *v.* 16th century. To play a quick round of hide the sausage, i.e. to have sex. From the standard English term for a young bullock. Used by Bill the Bard himself in *Othello*, when Iago tells Brabantio 'An old blacke Ram is tupping your white Ewe.'

TWAT *n.* The pussy; the honeypot. In continuous use since the 17th century. Also used as an insult, often for a stupid or cruel person.

VELVET *n.* 19th century. Tongue, also used to mean vagina. See also TO TIP THE VELVET.

VENUS' CURSE *n.* 19th century. Sexually transmitted disease. Venus is the goddess of love, and this term alludes to venereal disease being a curse that must be borne if someone is free with their love.

"TOWN BULL"
n. 17th century.
A promiscuous man.

WEDDING TACKLE *n.* 18th century. Penis. After the penis' use on the wedding night. Still in common usage. See also MARRIAGE GEAR.

WHIM-WHAM *n.* 18th century. Wham-bam; the sexual act. From quim meaning vagina, and wham, suggesting thrusting.

WHOREMONGER *n.* He who satisfies his hunger for laced mutton, i.e. a promiscuous man. In almost continuous usage since the 16th century.

WORST PART *n.* 16th/17th century. Vagina. A negative euphemism, employed by John Donne. See also BEST PART.

THE SACRED AND THE PROFANE

RELIGION
Or Cock and His Holy Business

COCK *n.* 14th century. The Man Upstairs, i.e. God. Directly compares God to the penis. Used by Chaucer and Old Bill, e.g. in *Hamlet*, when Ophelia sings to Claudius 'Young men will do't, if they come to't. By Cock, they are to blame.'

DAD-SNATCHED *adj.* 19th century. A variation on the theme of 'God-damned'.

EGAD *n.* 17th century. An exclamation akin to 'Oh God!'

FAMILY OF LOVE *n.* 16th century. A religious sect, sometimes called a cult, and also known by the German name Haus der Liebe, or Familia Caritatis. Also used as a mocking term for prostitutes, suggesting they are a close-knit group who provide 'love'.

GADZOOKS *n.* 17th century. An exclamation from either God's hooks, or God's hocks/hucks (God's hipbones). The latter would suggest this term references God's bones.

GODDAM *n.* 15th century. An exclamation meaning 'God damn'. Still in use.

GO TO HELL AND HELP YOUR MOTHER MAKE BITCH PIE! *phrase* 18th-century insult, insulting the recipient, their mother, and religion.

GO TO PUTNEY ON A PIG! *phrase* 19th century. An insult, meaning the same as 'Go to hell!' Provides a negative view of Putney and of pigs!

JIMINY CRICKETS *n.* 17th century. Used as an exclamation, meaning 'Jesus Christ'.

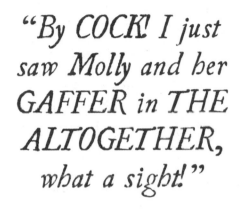

"By COCK! I just saw Molly and her GAFFER in THE ALTOGETHER, what a sight!"

COCK – God
GAFFER – Husband
THE ALTOGETHER – Nude

LAWKS *n.* 18th century. An exclamation derived from 'Lord', meaning either God or Jesus. Similar usage to 'for God's sake!'

PATRICO'S KINCHEN *n.* 16th century. Pig. Literally means 'priest's child', which makes some bold suggestions about priests' sexual habits.

SWEAR WORDS AND INSULTS
Or Cabbage-heads, Cheesecutters and Cuckoos

ADDLEPATE *n.* 18th century. A dunce; a ninny; a fool – one who is easily confused. Stems from the standard English word 'addle', meaning to confuse, and pate, which means head.

BARKER *n.* 15th century. A thug or ruffian, one who 'barks' threateningly. Also used to describe fairground touts, who bark out their offers.

BARMY *v*. 17th century. Loony; loopy; mad. To be barmy is to be crazy. From the standard English word 'barm', which means yeast, this term gives the impression of a mind bubbling over. Still in common usage.

BAT *n*. 18th century. A woman, often 'old bat' for an old woman. Also a prostitute.

BATS IN THE BELFRY *v*. 19th century. To have or to be bats in the belfry means to be insane or crazy. It suggests the brain is 'infested', which is why the person in question is mad. Still in use today, it has spawned many modern terms for crazy, including batty and batshit.

BEEF-WITTED *adv*. 16th century. Stupid, foolish. Suggests that the person in question has an intellect comparable to that of a cloven-hoofed bovine.

BERK *n.* 19th century. Shortened form of the rhyming slang *Berkshire Hunt*, meaning 'cunt'. Used as an insult for both men and women. Still in common usage, and often used without an understanding of its meaning.

BLABBERER *n.* 14th century. Someone who suffers from verbal diarrhoea; a person who talks too much, a chatterer. Commonly used by the writer John Wyclif, the term is related to the word 'blab', meaning chatter.

BOUNCER *n.* 17th century. A thug or violent person. This word is still in use, but has come to mean a doorman, though the brutish undertones still remain.

BUFFLEHEAD *n.* 17th century. A dunderhead; a half-wit. From the French for buffalo, *buffle*, This gives the impression of a thick skull, or indeed of horns, which were seen as a sign of stupidity or of a cuckold.

BUZZARD *n.* 14th century. A gullible and ignorant person. Also an ugly woman, usually an older one.

CABBAGE-HEAD *n.* 17th century. An idiot or fool. Suggests that the person in question has a brain as useless for thinking as the weighty, many-leafed vegetable.

CACAFUEGO *n.* 17th century. He who spouts hot, stinking lies; a braggart. The term literally means 'shit fire', making this an ancestor of the modern-day 'bullshitter' and 'bullshit artist'.

CAKE *n.* 18th century. An idiot. Suggests that the person in question is 'soft in the head' or 'improperly baked'.

CAN'T SEE A HOLE IN A LADDER – Piddled; a person who can't see a hole in a ladder is inebriated to the point of confusion and/or stupidity. 19th century.

CHANEY-EYED *adj.* 17th century. A person with small eyes, like a china doll. Also a person with glass eyes.

CHEESECUTTER *n.* 19th century. A nose that could double as an implement for slicing a nice block of cheddar, i.e. a very prominent nose, suggesting it is shaped similarly to a cheese knife.

"CLODPOLL"
n. 17th century.
An ignoramus.

COUSIN BETTY *n.* 19th century. A female fool. Also used to mean a prostitute.

CLODPOLL *n.* 17th century. A 'thick head'; an ignoramus. Clod suggests a thick, dense lump and poll here means head.

COW *n.* 18th century. A negative term for a woman. Started to be used as a synonym for prostitute in the 19th century. Still in common usage with the first definition.

CRACKED *v.* 17th century. To 'lose the plot', i.e. to become crazy. To be cracked is an abbreviated form of to be cracked in the head, suggesting an insane person is damaged.

CRACKPOT *n.* 19th century. A person whose 'dome' has suffered one too many blows, i.e. a fool. Still in common usage, though often to mean an insane person, or dangerously foolish one.

CUCKOO *n.* 17th century. An insane person. Can also be used as a verb, 'that person is cuckoo'. Used by Bill the Bard himself in 1600, in *Henry IV, pt. II.*

CUTTER *n.* 16th century. The earliest slang term for a braggart.

DOOLALLY *v.* 19th century. Originally coined by the British Indian Army, this comes from the term 'doolally tap', tap being Hindi for fever. It stems from the Deolali military sanatorium in Bombay (modern-day Mumbai), where troops with mental illness were sent. It has been claimed, however, that it was actually the place that sent people mad, rather than mad people being sent to the place.

DOTTY *adj.* 19th century. Imbecilic. Related to 'doddery', which means infirm or stumbling. Can also be used to describe a crazy person, and can be found in the faux-Latin intensifiers 'dottima' and 'dottissima'. Still in common usage, but often to mean being mad about something/someone, e.g. in the phrase 'they're dotty over that'.

EEJIT *n.* 19th century. A fool. A phonetic spelling of 'idiot', particularly with an Irish accent. Still in common usage.

FEATHER-BED AND PILLOWS *n.* 19th century. She who has extra padding in her soft and lumpy bits, i.e. a chubby woman. After her shape and the comfort a man would find lying with her.

FLY-TRAP *n.* Mouth. 18th century. Suggests a mouth held open in a dumb fashion by an idiot. The term 'catching flies' is still used to mean gaping with one's mouth wide open.

FOOLS WEDDING *n, pl.* 19th century. Negative term for a group of women. Related to the term 'mothers' meeting', which is still in use today.

"FUSTILUGS"
n. 17th century. A nasty or beastly woman.

FUSTILUGS *n.* 17th century. A nasty or beastly woman. Literally means 'dirty ears'.

TO BE GAGA *v.* 19th century. Crazy or insane. First used by Rudyard Kipling, and related to the French term *gateux*, meaning an old, feeble incontinent man. It also means drunk. Still in common use.

TO HAVE THE GIFT OF THE GOB *v.* 17th century. To be blessed in the region of one's waffle box, i.e. to have a wide mouth. Also used to suggest someone is articulate. By the 18th century, this had morphed into 'gift of the gab', and retained the second meaning. This version is still in use.

GIG *n.* 17th century. A flighty or fickle woman.

TO HAVE A SCREW LOOSE *v.* To be insane. In continuous use since the 19th century.

HEIFER *n.* 19th century. A negative term for a woman, often a woman of fuller figure. Still in use, but often with the spelling 'heffer', to mean a large, unattractive woman.

KNOW-IT-ALL *n.* 19th century. A person of intelligence, but often used in a derogatory manner, i.e. for one who thinks they are knowledgeable but shows off too much. Still in common usage.

LICKSPITTLE *n.* 18th century. A person who behaves obsequiously towards those in power. A toady.

LIGHTHOUSE *n.* 19th century. He whose nose is so bright red it could be used to guide ships through fog.

LONGEARS *n.* 19th century. A fool, an ass. Compares the idiot directly to a donkey with its long ears.

LOOBY *n.* 14th century. A fool. The earliest recorded slang term for an idiot, which also suggests a large physical presence, as well as stupidity. The modern term 'loopy', meaning foolish or insane, is derived from this.

LOONY *n.* 19th century. A fool. Suggests someone has been affected by the pull of the moon. Still in common usage, though usually referring to someone who is insane, or eccentric, rather than stupid.

LUBBER *n.* 14th century. A fool. Likely derived from the earlier LOOBY, this word later became part of the nautical phrase 'land-lubber', meaning a non-seafaring person.

LUMMOX *n.* 19th century. A clumsy person, one who moves around heavily. Suggests a large and ungainly individual. From the verb 'lummock', which means 'to move heavily or clumsily'.

MOP *n.* 19th century. A drunk. Also used to mean a drinking binge.

MOUTH ALMIGHTY *n.* 19th century. A person with an oversized, overused chatter box, i.e. a braggart, one who uses his mouth to his benefit. An extension of the 17th-century term 'mouth'.

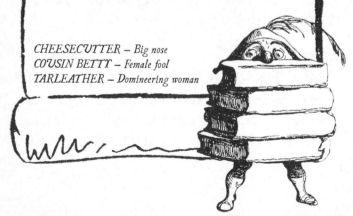

"*Did you see the CHEESECUTTER on that COUSIN BETTY? Might not be a looker, but at least she's no TARLEATHER!*"

CHEESECUTTER – Big nose
COUSIN BETTY – Female fool
TARLEATHER – Domineering woman

ASK MY NANCY *phrase* A 19th-century insult which means 'ask my anus'. The answer you would get would be wind, or faeces.

MUCKWORM *n.* 18th century. A miser, a skinflint.

NODDY *n.* 19th century. A fool, one who nods or wags his head.

NOODLE *n.* 18th century. A fool. Most likely from the term 'noddle', which means head, rather than related to the foodstuff.

NUMBSKULL *n.* 18th century. A fool or an idiot. A self-explanatory insult which is still in common usage.

"PESTLEHEAD"
n. 19th century.
An idiot.

TO BE OUT OF ONE'S NUT *v.* 19th century. To be insane. 'Nut' here refers to the head. Still in common usage, though usually in the newer form of 'to be off one's nut'.

PETTIFOGGER *n.* 16th century. A second-rate lawyer, one whose methods emulate the great successes, but whose work is at the lowest level.

PESTLEHEAD *n.* 19th century. An idiot or a fool. 'Pestle' is a phallic shape, and refers to the penis, making this term an ancestor of the modern 'dickhead', which is not only used to mean idiot, but also a nasty or aggressive person.

PILGARLICK *n*. 17th century. An outcast. Often seen as a 'poor pilgarlick', a pitiful creature. Derived from 'peel garlic'.

PILLOCK *n*. An idiot. 14th-century Northern dialect, originally meaning penis. Still in common usage.

PUDDING-BELLY *n*. 18th century. A fat person. One who has eaten too much spotted dick, etc., or, whose belly resembles a round pudding.

QUEER IN THE ATTIC *adj*. 19th century. Mad or drunk, the attic being the head, the highest part of the body.

RAGAMUFFIN *n.* 16th century. A disreputable, scruffy person. First appeared in the 14th century, in William Langland's poem *Piers Plowman*, as the name of a demon (spelt Ragamoffyn).

SAWNEY *n.* 17th century. A fool. From the 16th-century standard English term 'zany', which was often used to mean clown. 'Zany' is still in common use, though its derivatives are not.

TO SEE PINK ELEPHANTS *v.* 19th century. Phrase used to deride one who has unsuccessfully staved off the visual impairments induced by the consumption of alcohol; to be drunk to the point of confusion.

SHICER *n.* 19th century. A wastrel; a worthless individual. Possibly from the German *scheisse*, meaning shit, or from 'shice', meaning worthless.

SLUBBERDEGULLION *n.* 17th century. An undesirable. From the Dutch *overslubbern*, to wade through mud, and also 'slobber', to dribble, this term suggests a dirty, slobbering person, who is therefore not worth associating with.

SOP *n.* 17th century. A fool. From the standard English term 'milksop', which was derogatory in and of itself.

SQUINNY-EYES *n.* 17th century. A person with a squint.

STRUT-NODDY *n.* 19th century. An ignorant dunderhead who has no notion of their own idiocy, therefore struts around, thinking they are intelligent. See also NODDY.

SPARROW-MOUTH *n.* 19th century. Someone with an excessively large mouth. Most likely from the way that baby birds sit in the nest with their mouths wide open, waiting to be fed.

STUMP *n.* 19th century. An idiot. Like LOOBY, this suggests the physical as well as the intellectual, a stump being short and thick. Likely a precursor to the modern phrase 'as thick as two short planks'.

SUCK-BOTTLE *n.* 17th century. He who feeds feverishly from the wine bottle; an expert in self-intoxication; a drunk. From the verb 'to suck the bottle', meaning to drink.

SWEEP *n.* 19th century. An undesirable. Abbreviated from chimney sweep, likely because of their dirtiness. It is worth noting, however, that at certain times, especially at weddings, chimney sweeps were (and still are) considered good luck.

TARLEATHER *n.* 17th century. A domineering woman, one who scolds. Also used generally as an abusive term for a woman. From the standard English term which means a strip of leather which is used in a flail.

THATCH-GALLOWS *n.* 18th century. Someone so worthless they would only be good for thatching gallows (which have no roof!).

TORY *n.* 17th century. An outlaw or brigand. From the Irish *tóraidhe*, a pursuer. Still in use, though as a term for a member of the Conservative Party.

YAHOO *n.* 18th century. A hooligan, lout or philistine. First coined by Jonathan Swift in *Gulliver's Travels.*

YOB *n.* 19th century. A ruffian or unsavoury character. From the backslang for boy. Still in common usage, especially to mean a petty criminal.

CRIME AND PUNISHMENT

APPLE SQUIRE *n.* 16th century. A man who offers sweet, delectable things to a particular clientele, i.e. a pimp. Apple was a term for woman, and was later used to mean the vagina.

ARCH DOXY *n.* 17th century. A top female criminal, equivalent to the ARCH GONNOF. Doxy usually refers to a prostitute, but here is more generally used for criminal.

ARCH GONNOF *n.* 19th century. A top criminal, from the Yiddish term *gonnif*, meaning thief. See also ARCH DOXY.

ARK RUFFIAN *n.* 18th century. A river thief, 'ark' representing the boat from which they would work. See also WATERPAD.

"BLUDGER"
n. 19th century.
A violent thief or pimp.

BEAGLE *n.* 17th century. A police detective. One of the many words describing the police as animals. Detectives have always been described as various breeds of 'sniffer dog', for the way they sniff out crime. Went on to become bloodhound in the 19th century.

BLOCKHOUSE *n.* 17th century. Prison. Originally, the word referred to a fort. Using it for prison reiterated how hard it is to get out.

BLOODHOUND *n.* 19th century. Following on from the 17th-century BEAGLE, this describes police detectives as 'sniffer dogs'.

BLUDGER *n.* 19th century. A violent thief or pimp, who used a bludgeon as their weapon of choice.

BLUEBOTTLE *n.* 19th century. Policeman. Reversed slang term, as 'policeman' was first a slang term for a bluebottle fly, due to its colour, which is similar to a policeman's uniform.

BLUE PIGEON FLYER *n.* 18th century. A thief who stole lead from the roofs of houses. At the time, this lead was known as 'blue pigeon'.

BOBBY *n.* 19th century. Police officer. Like PEELER, this term was derived from Robert Peel's name. However, where *peeler* fell into disuse quite swiftly, *bobby* has remained a popular slang term for police officer, perhaps even used with some affection. One phrase in which it is still commonly heard is 'bobby on the beat', meaning a police officer who does rounds of an area.

BOOBY HUTCH *n.* 19th century. The loony bin; a mental hospital. Also used for a police station.

BUFFER NAPPER *n.* 17th century. A dog thief, from the 16th-century word 'bufe', meaning 'dog'. Also seen as simply 'buffer'.

BULLY-BUCK *n.* 18th century. A thief who would use violence to their advantage by deliberately causing fights between others, then robbing them during the confusion which followed. Also seen as 'bully-cock'.

BUTTOCK AND FILE *n, group*. 17th/18th century. A prostitute and a thief, working as a team. The prostitute would have sex with their chosen victim, and while he was distracted, the thief would rob him of his valuables.

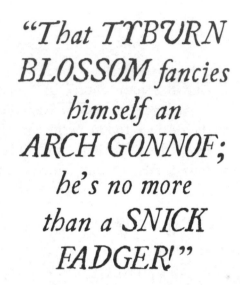

"*That TYBURN BLOSSOM fancies himself an ARCH GONNOF; he's no more than a SNICK FADGER!*"

TYBURN BLOSSOM – *Young thief*
ARCH GONNOF – *Top criminal*
SNICK FADGER – *Small-time thief*

BUTTOCK AND TWANG *n, group*. 17th century. Like **BUTTOCK AND FILE**, this was a prostitute and thief working in tandem. However, this team's work did not involve any sex; instead, the victim would be lured in by the prostitute's promise of satisfaction, and then the thief would beat and rob him.

CANARY *n*. 17th century. A convict; jail bird; a prisoner, from the fact that canaries were often kept in cages. Also seen as 'canary-bird'.

THE CANTING CREW *n*. 16th/17th century. Criminal beggars, who used 'cant' language, often seen as the basis for slang.

CAT AND KITTEN NIPPER *n.* 19th century. A thief, specialising not in stealing pets, but in thieving pewter tankards from taverns. The quart pot was known as a cat, and the pint pot as a kitten.

CHALDEE *n.* 17th century. Con artist. 'Chaldee' meant astrologer, suggesting they were trusted about as much as con artists. Indeed, many such conmen would purport to use astrology to 'benefit' their victims.

CLINK *n.* 16th century. The big house; prison. Originally referred to Southwark prison only, but soon became a general term, and is still in use as such.

CLOAK-TWITCHER *n.* 18th century. A thief who stole cloaks by quickly pulling ('twitching') them from their owners' backs. Also known as a 'silk-snatcher'.

CONEY-CATCHER *n.* 16th century. A conman. Based on the standard English word 'coney', which meant rabbit and has been in use since the 13th century. In this case, the 'coney' is the fool, ready to be swindled, and the 'coney-catcher' is the con artist who spots and catches them out. Details of their methods and tricks appeared for the first time in Robert Greene's *Art of Coney-Catching*.

COPPER *n.* 19th century. Police officer. Seen in the USA as 'cop', this term is derived from the Latin *capere*, which means 'to capture'. Still in common usage.

CUTPURSE *n.* 17th century. Like a pickpocket, the cutpurse stole valuables held on the person, but was less skilled, therefore cut the purse-strings and took the entire purse, rather than opening it and removing only the valuable items and/or money.

DIP *n.* 19th century. A pickpocket, for the way they 'dip' their hand into their victims' pockets to remove their valuables. Still in use.

DIVER *n.* 16th century. A small boy who is used as a thief's accomplice. He would climb through a small window, which an adult or even an older child would not be able to pass through, and then either let the rest of his crew in, or pass out the goods. Dickens' character Oliver Twist was employed for this sort of work.

DUBBER *n.* 17th century. A lock-pick, derived from 'dub' meaning lock.

DUDDER *n.* 18th century. A con artist who specialised in clothes ('duds'), selling them to dupes under the pretence of them being smuggled items, which they invariably were not. Also known as the 'whispering dudder' for the way their wares were sold 'on the quiet'.

"DIP"
n. 19th century.
A pickpocket.

DUFFER *n.* 18th century. Like the DUDDER, this con artist sold 'contraband' to dupes, but in the form of silks and brandies. Derived from 'duff', which itself means supposed contraband. The word 'duff' is still in common usage, meaning damaged, fake or second-rate goods.

FAMBLER *n.* 16th century. A purveyor of forgeries; a counterfeiter who makes rings ('fambles') which are meant to look and feel like gold, but are fake.

FIDLAM-BENS *n.* 18th century. A thief who will take anything at all, even if it has very little value.

FILE *n.* 18th century. Pickpocket, especially one who is skilled at the task.

FILCHING COVE *n.* 18th century. A thief who specialised in stealing the choicest of items using a 'filch', a long pole, so as not to be caught. The female equivalent is a 'filching mort'. As a verb, 'to filch' is still in usage, meaning to steal.

FIRE PRIGGER *n.* 18th century. A con artist and thief who specialised in swindling people whose houses were burning down. Pretending to help the people in their time of need, the fire prigger would take the opportunity to rob them of their belongings, taking advantage of the confusion caused by the fire, and the fact that the owners would not miss items they thought had simply been destroyed by fire. Also known as a 'tinny hunter', 'tinny' meaning fire.

"FOOTPAD"
*n. 18th/19th century.
A highway thief.*

FLEECY-CLAIMER *n.* 19th century. A sheep-napper, from the fleece of the sheep, and the way the thief laid claim to them.

TO FLOOR THE PIG AND BOLT *v.* Early 19th-century phrase meaning 'to knock down the police officer and run'.

FLOWERY *n.* 19th century. A prison cell. Short for 'flowery dell', which is rhyming slang for 'cell'.

FOOTPAD *n.* 18th/19th century. A highway thief, one who walks the 'pad', being the road or streets, looking for potential victims.

FORTY-POUNDER *n.* 19th century. Police officer. From the bonus received if a police officer caught a murderer.

GENTLEMAN OF THE PAD *n.* 18th/19th century. A tramp, a vagrant, and by association, a thief. 'Pad' in this sense means 'road', and comes from the Old German *pfad*, meaning path. With the tramp wandering the streets, even walking from town to town, the 'pad' was central to their identity. Also known as 'gentleman of the road'.

HEDGE CREEPER *n.* 17th century. Like the 16th-century LULLY PRIGGER, this thief stole people's linens. Named for how they would creep along the hedges, stealing the clean laundry from where it was left out to dry.

JUMP *n.* 18th century. A burglar, for the way they would jump through a window to enter and leave the house they were burgling.

KIDDY *n.* 19th century. A small-time pimp or thief, but one who probably thinks much of himself. Also a child. Still in common usage today with its second, less vulgar meaning.

LANDPIRATE *n.* 17th century. A scourge of the open road; a highwayman, for the way he steals from vessels. This term was commonly accepted as standard English.

LULLY PRIGGER *n.* 16th century. A thief who stole people's linens as they lay out to dry. See also HEDGE CREEPER.

MACER *n.* 18th century. A trickster and thief who would 'buy' goods on credit, but never get round to paying for them. Also known as a 'mace cove'. From the Yiddish terms *mos*, meaning to make money, and *masser*, meaning someone who betrays others.

MACKERAL *n.* 15th century. A pimp. From the French *maquereau* and the Dutch *makelaar*, which both mean 'to pander'.

TO GO MAY GATHERING *v.* 19th century. To go sheep stealing, from the fact that the lambs will be ready around May.

MOOCHER *n.* 19th century. A thief, beggar or vagrant. Also seen as a verb, 'mooch'. Still in common usage, not only for beggars but also for those who are out of work, or people who borrow from their friends and family.

MORK *n.* 19th century. A flatfoot; a bobby. Like ROZZER, this comes from Romany, specifically from the word *mooshkeroo*, which means constable.

MUMPER *n.* 17th century. Beggar. Also seen as a verb, 'mump', to beg. From the Dutch verb *mompen*, which means 'to cheat'.

NAMESCLOP *n.* 19th century. Backslang for policeman. Also seen as 'esclop', for police.

NASKIN *n.* 17th century. Prison. Also seen as 'nask', this term resulted in such names as the 'New Nask', referring to Clerkenwell prison.

NEWGATE NIGHTINGALE *n.* 18th century. A fledgling thief; a young criminal, for the fact that they were bound to end up in Newgate prison.

NIGHT-HUNTER *n.* 19th century. A thief who preferred to work under cover of darkness. Also known as a 'night bird', 'night-poacher', 'night-snap', and 'nighthawk' among others.

PEELER *n.* 19th century. Police officer. Named for Robert Peel, who was the Secretary for Ireland and set up the beginnings of the modern police force. This term was originally used for the Irish police only. It later came into use in the whole of Britain, but fell into disuse in most areas by the end of the 19th century. See also BOBBY.

PICARO *n*. 18th century. A cheat or gamester, from the Spanish word *picaro* meaning rogue. Also seen as picaroon.

PIG *n*. 19th century. A ROZZER; a police officer. An enduring term, showing a great deal of distaste for the police. Still in common usage, and considered one of the most offensive terms for the police.

READER-HUNTER *n*. 17th/18th century. A thief who specifically stole pocket books (readers).

RESURRECTION COVE *n*. 19th century. Grave robbers, who dug up bodies and then sold their wares to teaching hospitals. Also known as 'resurrection men', though this may be a later development. 'Resurrection' refers to the way they give the bodies they steal a 'second life' for medical experimentation.

RIVER RAT *n.* 19th century. A thief who would strip the dead bodies floating in the river Thames of their belongings.

ROARER *n.* 17th century. A 'muscle man' or thug, who acted as an accomplice to thieves.

ROBERD'S MAN *n.* 17th century. A thief, derived from Robin Hood.

"ROZZER"
n. 19th century.
Police officer.

ROOK *n.* 16th century. A cheat, from the bird's supposed tendency towards thievery. One of many animal terms for cheats. See also SHARK.

ROZZER *n.* 19th century. Police officer. Derived from the Romany language used by gypsies and traders, this term is still in use as a derogatory term for the police.

SAINT PETER'S SONS *n, pl.* 18th century. Thieves, from the way they 'hook' or 'angle'. Named after the Bible's Saint Peter, who was said to be the greatest of fishermen.

SATYR *n.* 18th century. A 'wild man', who made his living by stealing livestock, particularly cows. Based on the mythological creature of the same name.

"Had to set the ROARER on some snooping BLUE BOTTLE today. He caught me MAY GATHERING and I didn't fancy another term in the FLOWERY!"

ROARER *Heavy*
BLUE BOTTLE – *Policeman*
MAY GATHERING – *Sheep-stealing*
FLOWERY – *Prison cell*

SHARK *n.* 16th century. Someone who cheats at cards, an animal term for a cheat, akin to *rook*. The term 'card shark' is still in use.

SHIFTER *n.* 16th century. A conman who specialises in cheating young or unworldly tavern customers, by tricking them into paying for the shifter's dinner and drinks.

SKIPPER *n.* 16th century. A beggar, someone who is sleeping rough. During this period, 'rough' would usually have been in a barn, and this term is likely derived from *ysgubor*, a Welsh word meaning barn.

SKYLARKER *n.* 18th century. A burglar who also worked as a builder, and used this position to facilitate his crime. Called a 'lark' because he would rise early to set to work, finding vulnerable homes.

SNAKESMAN *n.* 19th century. The adult version of the 18th-century term 'little snakesman'. These thieves' accomplices were used, like the DIVER, to gain entry to people's homes so that they could be burgled. Rather than through a window, though, the snakesman would enter through a drain.

SNICK FADGER *n.* 19th century. A small-time thief. 'Snick' here means snatch, and 'fadger' is slang for farthing. This suggests such a thief would grab anything, even if it had very little value.

SNIDE PITCHER *n.* 19th century. A distributor of 'snide', counterfeit money. The word 'snide' is still in use, meaning fake or forged.

SPORTING HOUSE *n.* 19th century. A brothel. A place a man goes 'for sport'.

SQUIRE OF THE PETTICOAT *n.* 17th century. A pimp, petticoat being a general term for both women as a whole, and prostitutes.

STAG *n.* 18th century. Police detective. This is a classic reversal, common to slang, as stags are the prey, pursued in nature, whereas detectives do the chasing.

SWYGMAN *n.* 16th century. A wandering thief, one who posed as a pedlar. Likely derived from *swag*, meaning a heavy pack, which such a thief would no doubt have carried. Also seen spelt 'swigman'.

TEALEAF *n.* 19th century. Rhyming slang for 'thief'. Still in common usage.

'TEC *n.* 19th century. An abbreviation of 'detective', used to describe the new plain-clothes police who had entered the force in 1843.

TOY GETTER *n.* 19th century. A watch snatcher, 'toy' being a term for a pocket watch.

TYBURN BLOSSOM *n.* 18th century. A young criminal. Named for the gallows at Tyburn, the idea is that they will one day grow into the 'fruit', the bodies which swing from the gallows for their crimes.

WALKING POULTERER *n.* 18th century. A poultry thief, who would then walk door to door, trying to sell their wares.

WATERPAD *n.* 18th century. A river thief, this is the waterways' equivalent of the FOOTPAD. See also ARK RUFFIAN.

DEATH AND DISEASE

"CHATES"
n. 16th century.
Gallows.

TO BLESS THE WORLD WITH ONE'S HEELS *v.* 16th century. To be hanged, from the fact that the victim's feet would be waving around beneath them as they struggled, in a similar way to a priest waving a blessing over their devotees.

CHATES *n.* 16th century. Gallows. Also seen as 'chats' and 'chattes'. From the word 'cheat' meaning thing.

CLAP *n.* 16th century. Venereal disease, gonorrhoea in particular. Was standard English until around the 19th century, when it started to be considered vulgar and as such became a slang term. It is thought to have been developed from the French word *clapoir*, meaning bubo (pustule). Still in use, though usually more generally for any sexually transmitted infection, rather than specifically gonorrhoea; 'to have the clap' is to be infected with an STI.

COLD MEAT *n.* 18th century. A corpse, from the way the dead flesh becomes cold to the touch.

DEADLY NEVERGREEN *n.* 18th century. The gallows. Like the TYBURN TREE, this name compares the structure to the trunk and boughs of an evergreen, though of course it is 'nevergreen' as it will never grow.

TO DIE OF A HEMPEN FEVER *v.* 18th century. To die by hanging, 'hempen' referring to the material from which the noose was made.

FLAP DRAGON *n.* A sexually transmitted disease. Described by Grose as 'a clap, or pox', likely from 'flap' for genitalia, and 'dragon' for the dangerous burning of venereal disease. However, from the 16th to the 19th century, it was the name of a popular game, also known as snap-dragon.

FRENCH GOUT *n.* 18th century. Syphilis. The replacement for the 16th-century SPANISH NEEDLE, as Spain had been replaced by France as Britain's national enemy. Seen also as 'French goods', 'French crown' and the simple yet effective 'malady of France' and 'Frenchman'. 'French disease' was used as a term for syphilis, and as a general term for venereal disease. See also FRENCH PIG.

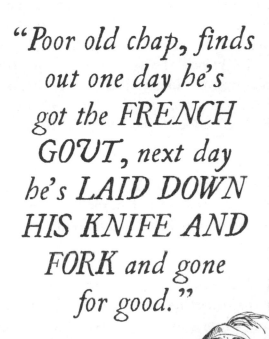

"*Poor old chap, finds out one day he's got the FRENCH GOUT, next day he's LAID DOWN HIS KNIFE AND FORK and gone for good.*"

FRENCH GOUT – *Syphilis*
LAID DOWN HIS KNIFE AND
FORK – *Died*

FRENCHIFIED *adj*. 17th century. Someone who is frenchified has been infected with venereal disease, which was commonly known as 'the French disease', showing the Brits' distaste for the French, and the way they were viewed as a sexual, even lewd, people. See also FRENCH GOUT and FRENCH PIG.

FRENCH PIG *n*. 18th century. A bubo, usually one associated with a sexually transmitted disease, such as FRENCH GOUT.

GLEET *n*. 18th century. Gonorrhoea, named for the discharge men with the disease will have, which looks like pus. From the Old French word *glette*, which means filth or slime.

HEMPEN NECKTIE *n*. 18th century. The hangman's noose, for the fact it was made of hempen rope, and the way it was wound round the victim's neck, like a tie.

HORSE *n*. 19th century. A sexually transmitted disease. 'Horse and trap' in full, this is rhyming slang for 'clap'. Also seen as rhyming slang for 'crap'.

TO KEEL OVER *v*. 19th century. To meet your Maker; to bite the big one; to die. Originally a seafaring term, this came to be used more generally, and is still in use.

TO KICK THE BUCKET *v*. 16th century. To expire. One of the most enduring slang terms for death, this is still in common usage.

TO LAY DOWN ONE'S KNIFE AND FORK *v*. 19th century. To finish one's dinner and leave the table for good, i.e. to die. From the fact that the dead have no need for bodily pleasures such as food.

TO MOUNT THE LADDER *v.* 16th century. To be hanged. 'Ladder' here means the gallows.

NUBBING *n.* 17th century. Hanging, 'nub' being the neck.

PICKLES *n.* 19th century. Corpses – used by medical students to describe dead bodies brought to them for dissection, parts of which would be pickled for study. Also seen as 'dead pickles'.

TO POP OFF *v.* 18th century. To reach the end of one's mortal coil; to die. Still in use, though more often to mean 'go away' or 'go somewhere'.

POX *n.* 16th century. Syphilis. Although used in conjunction with other words to denote diseases which create pocks on the body, such as smallpox and chicken pox, 'pox' on its own specifically refers to syphilis. It was, however, used interchangeably with CLAP, for sexually transmitted diseases in general. Was standard English until the 18th century, from when it was considered vulgar and therefore became a slang term.

"SCABBADO"
n. 17th century.
Syphilis.

SCABBADO *n.* 17th century. Syphilis. A version of the standard English word 'scab', made to look Spanish. For the way the pocks would scab over after they burst. See also SPANISH NEEDLE.

SCRAG 'EM FAIR *n.* 18th century. Public execution (by hanging), which was a popular form of entertainment, making it like a fair.

SCRAGGING POST *n.* 18th century. The gallows, 'scrag' being the neck.

TO SHAKE A CLOTH IN THE WIND *v.* 18th century. To be hanged. By the 19th century this had also come to mean to drink (alcohol), especially in the navy.

TO SLING ONE'S HOOK *v.* 19th century. To die. Like TO KEEL OVER, this was originally a seafaring phrase which came into common usage. It is still used today, but with a softer meaning of 'to go away'. The phrase 'Sling your hook!' means 'Go away!'

SPANISH NEEDLE *n.* 16th century. Syphilis. Also seen as 'spanish pox' and 'spanish gout'. This term shows up Spain as Britain's national enemy at the time. They would, however, come to be replaced by France by the 18th century. See also FRENCH GOUT.

STIFF'UN *n.* 19th century. A corpse, from the way rigor mortis makes the body stiffen. Also seen as simply 'stiff', which is still in use.

TO TAKE AN EARTH BATH *v.* 19th century. To lay down and get comfortable in your wormy bed, i.e. to expire. References the corpse being buried in the earth.

TOT *n.* 19th century. A bone, from the German meaning 'death'.

TOWER HILL VINEGAR *n.* 16th century. The swordsman's block, from when beheading was a common form of capital punishment, carried out at Tower Hill.

TYBURN TREE *n.* 17th century. Gallows. From the shape of them, with boughs like a tree, as well as the fact they were made from wood. Tyburn was the most infamous gallows location, by the Tyburn river in what is now London's Marble Arch.